Made
in
America

Made in America

The Shaping of Modern American Evangelicalism

Michael Scott Horton

A CURE Book

BAKER BOOK HOUSE
Grand Rapids, Michigan 49516

Printed in the United States of America

Horton, Michael Scott.
    Made in America : the shaping of modern American evangelicalism /
Michael S. Horton.
        p.   cm.
    ISBN 0-8010-4354-9
    1. Evangelicalism—United States. 2. Christianity and culture.
I. Title.
BR1642.U5H675   1991
270.8'29—dc20   91-9775
                                                                        CIP

Scripture references are from the Holy Bible, New International Version. Copyright © 1973, 1978, 1984 International Bible Society. Used by permission of Zondervan Bible Publishers.

CURE is the logo for
Christians United for Reformation
2568 E. Riles Circle
Anaheim, CA 92806

Christians United for Reformation is a parachurch group whose primary purpose is to bring about in America nothing less than a New Reformation. Through conferences, a radio program, a newsletter, and its books, CURE promotes Reformation theology, critiques evangelicals who have departed from it, and encourages atheological evangelicals to understand, embrace, and promote it.

Contents

84199

Introduction

The Emperor Has No Clothes

> It is Evangelicalism in the name of Evangelicalism
> that is destroying Evangelicalism.
> —Francis A. Schaeffer

The story is familiar to most of us. An emperor, jealous to have the most splendid robe of any monarch, commissioned the realm's designers to create a garment worthy of him and promised to execute designers who failed him.

Finally, the emperor's own tailor announced the completion of the realm's finest robe. But before opening the jewel-studded chest, the tailor informed the emperor and his court that the robe could be visible only to those who had wisdom. Unwilling to be regarded as lacking in wisdom, the emperor began laughing in approval of the invisible garment. Eventually, the whole court joined in and it was clear that the emperor's charge was met with impeccable success.

The next day, the emperor paraded his new robe through the streets. Informed beforehand that only those with wisdom could see the new robe, the people cheered wildly in approval. All was well until a child stepped forward. "But there's nothing there!" he exclaimed. "The emperor has no clothes!" Immediately, cheers turned to silence as the crowd descended upon the naive and hapless youth.[1]

Since first hearing that story I've often wondered why the people were so full of conviction about something that they knew was untrue. How were they duped into mistaking folly for wisdom and naïveté for sophistication?

I've also wondered in recent years when it will be safe to break the news, "The emperor has no clothes!" Perhaps it will never be safe. Until the struggle against abortion began to gain considerable support, Francis Schaeffer was considered a menace. He warned us about undermining evangelical Christianity in the name of evangelicalism.[2] Others have pointed out the ersatz, shallow character and content of much of contemporary Christianity. Nevertheless, it seems that the movement once known by the slogan "Reformed and always reforming according to the Word of God" has calcified into a bare conservatism that eschews correction and is too proud for self-examination.

The evangelical establishment has enjoyed worldly success: numbers, press coverage, political power, and material prosperity—so much so that it is easier to cheer for the new robe than to make a stir. Fearing the worst if flaws are confessed, we often miss opportunities to reform the church.

But Christianity is true. Its truth rests on historical facts which do not change, truths which are open to the tests normally applied to any other events or claims. If the success of Christianity depends on whether it can sell, or whether it works, or whether it feels good or provides meaningful experiences, then that success is threatened by exposure to the critical judgment of Scripture, not to mention of life's daily pressures. But our faith is true for different reasons—in the ultimate sense, that what Christianity teaches is the correct explanation of reality. If Christianity is true in that sense, a book like this one can hardly be considered a menace.

Like the medieval church, modern evangelicalism often uses the principle of unity to silence its critics. "Make every effort to keep the unity of the Spirit through the bond of peace," the apostle Paul commanded (Eph. 4:3), and this has been taken to mean that doctrinal discussions or debates are dangerous. Hence, we are urged to base our unity on a common experience (being "born again") which is usually reduced to such phrases as, "Invite Jesus into your heart," or "Accept Jesus as Savior," or "Let Jesus take control." We rest our koinonia (fellowship) on slogans and ideas which are foreign to the Bible, but which serve as signs that we are insiders and can therefore be trusted. To our bumper sticker, "Jesus Is the Answer," the world has justly countered with its own: "If Jesus Is the Answer, What's the Question?" For both questions and answers, we need correct thinking. And correct thinking requires criticism.

What did the apostle mean, then, when he told us to "make every effort to preserve the unity of the Spirit through the bond of peace"? First, he reminds us that we are one because of "one hope . . . , one Lord, one faith, one baptism" (Eph. 4:4–5). What is our common hope but a confession of faith: "I believe in the forgiveness of sins, the resurrection of the body, and the life everlasting"? And how can we have unity unless we are worshiping the One clearly described in the sacred text? The next requirement for unity is one faith. Is there such a thing as unity when we do not have a common faith—in other words, a common creed? Can we be baptized into one body regardless of what we believe about God, ourselves, salvation, or the person of Christ? Obviously not, and the apostle makes this clear in verses 13–14: "until we all reach unity *in the faith* [in the teachings of Christ] and *in the knowledge of the Son of God* and *become mature*, attaining to the whole measure of the fullness of Christ. *Then,*" he assures us, "we will no longer be infants, tossed back and forth by the waves, and blown here and there by every wind of teaching . . . " (italics added).

What held that group of early Christians together as they

faced martyrdom? What could have possibly driven people from diverse backgrounds to share a common death? It wasn't a common experience. Each became a Christian in a different way—some had immediate, others gradual, conversions. It wasn't a common language or culture—they were at odds with their culture. The only thing that could hold a group like that together in the face of massive pressures was a set of common convictions; in short, a common creed. As the church understood more fully what the Bible said, it began to define more clearly the basis of unity among Christians. The Nicene, Chalcedonian, Athanasian, and Apostles' creeds were written for this purpose.

Today, the World Council of Churches tells us, "Doctrine divides; service unites." And yet, a top-level official of that body told me that the council had come to recognize the opposite: "When you actually get out there on the field, you realize that it's doctrine that unites." He continued, "We come together when we talk about the great affirmations of the creeds; it's when you begin to work out practical strategies on the field that you discover disunity." While the World Council of Churches may or may not be discovering the bankruptcy of its past neglect of doctrine in favor of a contentless unity, is it possible that evangelicals are marching down the same dead-end street? Perhaps for us, it is "Doctrine divides; experience unites," or a similar formula, but historic Christianity does not allow us to accommodate superficial unity.

Eyeing the false prophets who preached prosperity and ignored truth, the prophet Jeremiah conveyed God's warning: "They dress the wound of my people as though it were not serious. 'Peace, peace,' they say, when there is no peace" (Jer. 6:14). Even if truth were not the basis for unity, our alternative foundations have not secured it. George Marsden, a professor at Duke University, notes, "The structure is somewhat like that of the feudal system of the Middle Ages. It is made up of superficially friendly, somewhat competitive empires built up by evangelical leaders competing for the same audience, but all professing allegiance to the same king."[3] One reads of the church in Laodicea words from Christ which strike close: "You say, 'I am rich; I have acquired wealth and do not need a thing.' But you do not realize that you are wretched, pitiful, poor, blind and naked" (Rev. 3:17).

Countless articles in Christian magazines and books and numerous features on Christian radio and television tell us how evangelicalism is booming, brimming with enthusiasm and excitement. We have our own networks, publishing companies, advertising agencies, amusement parks, and cruises! "But you do not realize that you are wretched, pitiful, poor, blind and naked."

The successes of evangelical marketing have even been characterized as a revival. Nevertheless, according to pollsters George Barna and William P. McKay, "Despite the millions of dollars spent on media ministry and evangelistic publishing, there has been no real growth in the size of the Christian population in the last five years."[4]

The year 1976 was not only our nation's bicentennial celebration, but, according to *Newsweek*, "The Year of the Evangelical." Credited with the election and re-election of conservative Ronald Reagan, the movement captured headlines as self-confident preachers informed us that God would make America preeminent again if we would follow their instructions. God became something of a mascot for the Republican Party until very recently, as the more moderate George Bush failed as a figurehead. While the hopes of voting in the kingdom of God and legislating its supposed agenda seem to have yielded to more pragmatic concerns, the ideologues continue to lead cell groups across the country.

Now, says pollster Louis Harris, the American people are distrustful of many religious figures in public life, a sentiment undoubtedly fueled by scandals involving both those the evangelicals elected to public office and some of the most prominent evangelical media preachers themselves.[5]

According to a prestigious research group, Oxford Analytica, the presumed religious revival lacks substance: "Despite impressive statistics and the appearance of surprising vitality, there is evidence that the state of religion in America is not quite what it appears. Almost all the statistical indicators on religion are up," the group reports. "But indicators of the social influence of religion are down."[6]

The myths of power, popularity, and growth have led to an unhealthy preoccupation with superficial success, methods over message, technique over truth, quantity over quality. A historian at the University of Chicago, Martin E. Marty, counsels, "Pure religion demands accurate stories. There should be no illusions. We dare not call ourselves one thing and be another. If we wish to follow religious visions, we have to know something about the odds, the distractions, the opposition. Americans are to be most faulted when they find religious justifications for their illusions and their worldly ways, when they are content with false prophets who tell them that they are spiritual when they are not."[7]

The Bible commands, "Do not conform any longer to the pattern of this world, but be transformed by the renewing of your mind" (Rom. 12:2). While much fuel has been spent on trying to get people to act like Christians, the Bible insists that we must first think like Christians. The transforming of our minds takes place not through magic, superstitious techniques, or superficial devotions, but through serious and sometimes difficult study. It requires that we know something about the Bible and the people to whom it is addressed, and that we know something about ourselves and the culture in which we live. It is dangerous to pretend one is not worldly when one refuses to critically examine the ways in which one has been influenced more by the spirit of the age than by the Spirit of Christ.

Donald G. Bloesch laments, "What is conspicuous in American church life in particular is the dissipation of doctrinal and apostolic substance. There is a preoccupation with the cultivation of the inner life and holistic salvation, but faithfulness to the apostolic faith, rediscovered and attested anew in the Reformation is dismally lacking."[8] The crisis of truth in our time, even in the evangelical church, is indeed serious. And it is due in part to our cultural accommodation.

It is the purpose of this book, therefore, to examine the relationship between the biblical teachings and the contemporary realities shaping who we are as American evangelicals. It is not my intention to be a cavalier or clever cynic, but to join my brothers and sisters on a pilgrimage back to an evangelicalism that is both in theory and in practice a worthy successor to the apostolic faith. "The evangelical faith," according to Bloesch, is "the historic Christian faith grounded in apostolic witness, reaffirmed by Augustine in his battle with Pelagius, and rediscovered by the Reformers and the Puritans. Such an evangelicalism must be clearly distinguished from the ideological or cultural evangelicalism that is so pervasive in America today."[9] Then, this volume will attempt to contrast authentic evangelicalism with the less authentic variety.

Let us hope for a day in the not-too-distant future when the world sees a humble church that no longer shelters hypocrisy, that no longer offers stones of legalism when the world needs the bread of life; a church that bids the world, "Come now, let us reason together" (Isa. 1:18) instead of expecting national awakening on the basis of slogans, shallow assertions, and unfounded myths. Let us hope that the time has run out for being "at ease in Zion." Let us pray for the day when the Christian community will no longer patronize the supermarket of pop religion, when there will be a recovery of passionate, warm-hearted orthodoxy and historic continuity, not with American legends, but with Christian truths.

Making God Safe for Democracy 1

> The Revolutionary could no more admit a sovereign
> God than he could a sovereign king. . . . Rulers
> henceforth rule only by the consent of the governed.
> The God of Puritanism, stripped of His antique pow-
> ers, had no recourse but to enter as a weakened
> prince into the temple of individualism and there to
> seek refuge.
> —Richard Mosier, *The American Temper*

Ever since Adam shifted the blame to Eve, pointing fingers has been a nasty habit of human nature.

Many theses on secularism have been proposed. Harvey
Cox argues that modern religion was born when "God, the
maker of heaven and earth, became the deity of religion,
approached through what came to be called 'religious experiences.'" Thus, "a faith which had once proclaimed a Lord
who lifted up and cast down emperors, who condemned
extortion and profit gouging, was now reduced to being
concerned exclusively with the inner spirit or at most
with frictions between individuals." Cox quotes Friedrich

15

Nietzsche: "You have caged [God], tamed him, domesticated him, and the priests have pliantly lent their aid. The roaring bull has become a listless ox. You have gelded God!'"[1]

It was perhaps as easy as it was natural for Nietzsche, a philosopher, to blame Christians themselves for the "death" of God. But before we judge too hastily, is it possible that the analysis has much to commend it? I think so.

John W. Whitehead's *The Stealing of America* expressed the growing resentment of the Christian right that our nation, established by the founding fathers upon Judeo-Christian principles, has been stolen by secular humanists who would silence all religions but their own.[2] Of course, the secular left often does hypocritically imagine that theirs is the only real truth, while they deny such claims of objectivity to others. Nevertheless, is this version of secularization, perhaps the most popular in evangelical circles, accurate? In this chapter I will argue that we evangelical Christians are culpable in the degeneration of religious vitality in our social, civic, and cultural life. It is secularized Christians rather than secular humanists who must account for the disintegration of religious vitality.

We are all secularized every day in ways we do not easily notice. I am constantly puzzled at the remarkable objectivity I have in criticizing individuals or actions around me, but I become remarkably tolerant of my own shortcomings. We have blind spots. By gaining historical perspective, however, we come to recognize those spots more readily. By bringing the rascals within us out into the open, we are better prepared to expose secularizing tendencies.

Before we can be honest in this matter, we must get rid of myths. Myths help us live with secularization. (For instance, many conservative Protestants in the early nineteenth century invented the idea that African-Americans were remnants of the cursed seed of Ham. Of course, nothing in the Bible lent support to the myth, but it was powerful. It was a religious way of justifying evil.) The myth we expose in this chapter is a popular one and it, too, has impeded an authentic Christian witness. It holds that

America was a born-again country at its founding in 1776 but lost its way as recently as the revolutionary 1960s and the subsequent two decades of license. According to this viewpoint, America was a promised land, originally dedicated to Jesus Christ, but now largely lost.

Is America a promised land, stolen by secular humanists? Has there *ever* been another nation so dedicated to the Lord? The Bible describes one theocratic promised land—an earthly Israel foreshadowing a heavenly Jerusalem. But the myth motivates us to become part of a movement to repair a chosen nation. During the last two decades the rhetoric about a God who had been ejected from classrooms and courtrooms drew heavily on the theme of recovering the promised land. Thus, in this scenario, secularization is blamed on secular humanists.

The idea of a Christian America is mythical not only in biblical prophesy but also in history. There never was a time since our founding as a nation when the republic was self-consciously Christian, in the biblical sense. This chapter will offer a brief historical sketch of our nation's religious heritage in an effort to identify the seeds of secularization. This historical summary will also serve as the background for discussions in following chapters.

"A Shining City upon a Hill"

In 1693, Cotton Mather defined the purpose of the New England settlers: In addition to enlarging the English empire, the "errand into the wilderness" also "afforded a singular prospect of churches erected in an American corner of the world, on purpose to express and pursue the Protestant Reformation."[3] John Winthrop called the experiment "a shining city upon a hill." The biblical realism of the Puritan's view of the sinful condition was balanced by the biblical optimism of divine sovereignty and grace. All of life was spiritual, a seamless fabric integrating heart, soul, body, and mind in an effort to live life *coram Deo* (in the presence of God). The kingdom of Christ was not confined to private devotions or church gatherings, but extended into all realms of human knowledge and activity.

The first Puritan settlers, along with the Plymouth Separatists who sailed to America on the *Mayflower*, were Calvinists who had sought further reformation of the Church of England than the Elizabethan Settlement would allow. Dubbed "Puritan" for their rigorous doctrinal and liturgical purity, many of these people grew impatient with the promises of reform while outspoken Puritan ministers were being deprived of salaries and others were jailed.

Anything but ascetic and world-denying, the Puritans felt at home in this world, viewing their role as reformers and improvers of the human condition. C. S. Lewis points out the popular misconceptions of the Puritans: "Whatever they were, they were not sour, gloomy, or severe, nor did their enemies bring such charges against them." In fact, according to the sainted defender of Roman Catholicism, Sir Thomas More, a Protestant was one "drunk of the new mist of lewd lightness of mind and vain gladness of heart," one who joined the Reformation because the Reformers "spiced all the poison with liberty." Lewis further describes the Puritans:

> Calvin, the great successful doctrinaire who had actually set up the "new order," was the man who had dazzled them all. We must picture these Puritans as the very opposite of those who bear that name today: as young, fierce, progressive intellectuals, very fashionable and up-to-date. They were not teetotallers; bishops, not beer, were their special aversion. And humanists in this context means simply "classicists." There was no necessary enmity between Puritans and humanists. They were often the same people, and nearly always the same sort of people: the young men "in the Movement," the impatient progressives demanding a "clean sweep."[4]

At the core of Puritan thought and life (for the two were held together) was the conviction that God is sovereign and that humans exist for no other purpose than "to glorify God and enjoy him forever." Whether puzzling over a piece of the new science or tasting the newly arrived sherry, the Puritan looked for ways to raise his eyes toward heaven in gratitude. God was in charge. He had elected his citizens and, while the earthly city was to be much more representative than England, the City of God was nothing short of a dictatorship. God's will ruled in both good and ill fortune; even in tragedy, God was glorified, and that was all the Puritan needed to go on with life.

Within the next few generations, however, the American experiment was to unravel and ultimately fail—if one measures success by the standards of the original Puritan vision. By the time of the War of Independence, the biblical and theological substance of the first American Protestants was compromised to such an extent that only secularized versions of the work ethic, an appreciation for culture and learning, and a sense of republican obligation and virtue remained. Let us look, then, at the turning point in Puritan America.

The Half-Way Covenant

With the other Reformers, John Calvin knew that the church could never be perfectly reformed. To say otherwise would contradict the clear teaching of Scripture and the Reformers themselves that Christians are simultaneously sinful and justified. Calvin, for instance, made a distinction between the visible and invisible church—the former consisting of all baptized Christians; the latter, of the elect alone. Although some signs are occasionally discernible, it is often a tenuous task to judge the elect by outward appearances. The Genevan Reformer wrote that "we are commanded to revere and keep communion with the latter" (members of the visible church) rather than inspecting their credentials. "To know who are His," says Calvin, "is a prerogative belonging solely to God." A caution follows: "For those who seemed utterly lost and quite beyond hope are by His goodness called back to the way while those who more than others seemed to stand firm often fall. Therefore, according to God's secret predestination (as Augustine says), 'many sheep are without, and many wolves are within.'"[5]

By contrast, Puritans in the 1630s considered visible signs of conversion a prerequisite for church membership. (This seems odd to modern evangelicals, for whom conversion has almost replaced justification, but it was an innovation in its day.) In America particularly, rigorous tests were applied to discern the elect; eventually moralism began to infect New England theology, more so as morals declined. As the Puritans began to lose their central focus—the gospel of grace—and allowed their reformist impulse to create a salvation by personal and social improvement, Christianity became the social glue: urbane, civil, and less concerned with theology.

For the early settlers of New England, there was no tension between being a member of the city of man and the City of God. To be a member of the body politic one had to be a member in good standing of the church. But now, as scores of unconverted heirs filled the population centers in and around Boston, accommodations were made. In 1662, just thirty years after conversion was required for church membership, communion was opened "to all moral persons whether or not they were regenerate."[6] The Half-Way Covenant allowed unconverted citizens to bring their children for baptism, providing their lives were not dissolute and they upheld the basic tenets of New England faith. Mather considered withholding baptism from those who could not confess to having had a conversion "a most unwarrantable strictness, which would quickly abandon the biggest part of our country to heathenism."[7] In no more than three decades, a rigorous test for conversions gave way to (some might say produced) accommodation to a largely civil religion. A piece of historical irony, the Puritan Commonwealth had become the very establishment it criticized in England. The Elizabethan Settlement was replaced with the Half-Way Covenant.

The way was now prepared for citizens to be more easily admitted to the city of man. But the more easily one could be admitted to the city of man, the easier his admission to the City of God. In thirty years the Puritans had reduced the vision of a "shining city upon a hill" to an unattainable ideal, settling instead for a civil religion.

Arminianism

This, however, was only the beginning of the apostasy. At Harvard, scholars began entertaining unorthodox notions about human nature and salvation which compromised Puritan thought and piety.

"The salt of the nations," as the Puritans called it, Harvard was founded in 1636 to ensure a learned clergy and hence, laity. By 1707, there were growing suspicions that Harvard was tolerating the unorthodox theories of James Arminius (1560–1609), a Dutch theologian whose followers found the Reformers' insistence on *sola gratia* (grace alone) restrictive of human will and potential. According to Peter Gay's celebrated work, *The Rise of Modern Paganism,* "In Arminius's sermons, Calvinism is softened to gentle instruction designed to lead sinful men toward a reform of their lives."[8] A celebrated case in 1735 involved Robert Breck, a Harvard graduate, who was charged with Arminianism by the regional council of pastors. "Before the middle of the century," according to Richard Hofstadter, "Arminianism was openly espoused by respectable ministers. Outcries against Arminianism, though often not technically correct, thus had a certain truth: the truth that many New Englanders had ceased to believe in their beliefs."[9]

The orthodox decided Harvard was no place for their youth, so off to Yale they went. The orthodoxy act gave the scholars of the college permission to examine fellow professors suspected of Arminianism.

In 1757, the Reverend Samuel Webster, a Harvard graduate, wrote *A Winter-Evening's Conversation upon the Doctrine of Original Sin,* in which he rejected the biblical teaching that the sinful condition is inherited by all because of Adam's fall (in other words, the idea that we are sinners even

apart from our own personal transgressions). All of this led
to a series of controversies and much ink was spilled in the
process.

Eventually, as Arminianism weakened the evangelical
and Reformed doctrines of sin and grace, it was blended
with Arianism, an ancient heresy denying Christ's eternal
deity. Attacking the doctrine of the Trinity, Jonathan May-
hew wrote, "Christians ought not, surely, to pay any such
obedience or homage to the Son as has a tendency to
eclipse the Glory of God the Father who is without Rival or
Competitor."[10] Before long, this blend of Arminianism and
Arianism became known as Unitarian-Universalism, and
Harvard to this day is known officially as a university in this
tradition. Many of Boston's leading Congregationalist
churches, once bastions of Puritan orthodoxy, became
citadelsof the Unitarian heresy.

The Enlightenment

As Arminianism shifted emphasis from the sovereignty of
God to a more positive view of human potential, a new
storm was darkening the horizon: the Enlightenment.
Ignobled by contradicting not only the church (as the
Reformers had done), but also the Bible, the architects of
the Enlightenment placed their own reason where revelation had been enthroned.

The average unbeliever today is likely to have the
impression that to be a thinking person, it is unreasonable
to be fettered by religious dogma, especially by the Bible.
But it is important that we realize that this perception is
due in part to our having accepted the divorce between the
heart and mind—a divorce which the Puritans, like the
Reformers before them, refused to recognize. It is difficult
for us to appreciate the harmony of intellect, emotion, and
reform that Reformation Christianity enjoyed. Thoughts
had inspired Reformers and Puritans, shaping their outlook,
affections, and activities in the community. "My heart is
stirred by a noble theme," sang the psalmist. Great thoughts

produced great emotions and both created motivation for reform in the surrounding world.

Furthermore, the Reformation produced some of the keenest minds and most of the great intellectual centers of our nation. In his Pulitzer Prize–winning book, *Anti-Intellectualism in American Life*, Richard Hofstadter notes, "The Puritan clergy founded the tradition of New England intellectualism; and this tradition, exported wherever New Englanders settled in large numbers, was responsible for the remarkably large portion of the country's dynamic intellectual life throughout the nineteenth century and on into the twentieth."[11] The dynamism of American intellectual life, perhaps, but the content was neutralized before the Revolutionary War.

"It is doubtful," Hofstadter remarks, "that any community ever had more faith in the value of learning and intellect than Massachusetts Bay."[12] Moses Coit Tyler, a distinguished literary historian, identifies Puritan priorities:

> In its inception New England was not an agricultural community, nor a manufacturing community, nor a trading community: it was a thinking community; an arena and mart for ideas. . . . Theirs was a social structure with its corner-stone resting on a book. . . . Only six years after John Winthrop's arrival in Salem harbor, the people of Massachusetts took from their own treasury the fund from which to found a university; so that while the tree-stumps were as yet scarcely weather-browned . . . , they had made arrangements by which even in that wilderness their young men could at once enter upon the study of Aristotle and Thucydides, of Horace and Tacitus, and the Hebrew Bible.[13]

Hofstadter adds, "Puritanism, as a religion of the Book, placed a strong emphasis upon interpretation and rational discourse and eschewed ranting emotionalism. Puritan sermons combined philosophy, piety, and scholarship; and it was one of the aims of Puritan popular education to train a laity capable of understanding such discourses." He concludes, "In the early days, at least, this seems to have been achieved."[14] The clergy assumed responsibility for a literate culture; such an assumption shows the gulf between the profound substance of Puritan sermons and some of the modern inspirational pep talks which pass for sermons, their chief intellectual wrestling consisting of a search for words that rhyme.

When evangelicals gave up Calvinistic orthodoxy, they abandoned an intellectual system which provided families, churches, communities, cities, schools, and trades with a way of looking at the world—a biblical way of doing so. With advancing knowledge and information, we no longer have a scheme for understanding how each piece of information relates to the larger view of the world. The results of this Enlightenment fragmentation are summarized in the comments of Jewish philosopher Will Herberg:

> The problem of the social order is a problem that in essence is theological and metaphysical. It is the theological and metaphysical tradition that has provided the sustaining armature of Western culture. But the spiritual armature of our culture . . . has reached an advanced state of disintegration. We are surrounded on all sides by the wreckage of our great intellectual tradition. In this kind of spiritual chaos, neither freedom nor order are possible. Instead of freedom, we have the all-engulfing whirl of pleasure and power; instead of order, we have the jungle wilderness of normlessness and self-indulgence.[15]

Historians have called this period the Age of Reason. In France, the divorce between reason and revelation was vividly displayed in the removal of the cross and all Christian symbols from the Cathedrale de Notre Dame. A massive statue of the goddess of reason was set in the void. Dogmatic (i.e., doctrinal) religion, said the French Enlightenment leaders, is an impediment to real progress. Man, unaided, is the answer to his own problems.

Voltaire in *Candide* cringed at the notion that a cosmic divine plan accounts for all things, even pain and suffering. With the Reformation, Voltaire announced, "a corner of the veil was lifted. The nations, aroused, wanted to judge what they worshipped."[16] But, said he, "I have done more in my own time than Luther and Calvin. I am tired of hearing it declared that twelve men sufficed to establish Christianity and I want to prove to them that it only needs one to destroy it."[17] (It has been pointed out with some delight that a Bible society is now housed in Voltaire's home.) Whether one emphasized human volition (Arminianism) or human reason (Enlightenment deism), this was the birth of secularism indeed.

Unaided human reason, not divine revelation, would dictate truth. That was not to say that religion was altogether unnecessary. Quite the contrary! It was essential for providing morality and sentiment. It was a sign of good manners to see the children praying . . . to whomever. With classical Greek and Roman civilization as their model, the Enlightenment thinkers sought to neuter Christianity without fatally wounding it.

It is essential that we realize that in this era America was born as a nation. Thomas Paine, Thomas Jefferson, and Benjamin Franklin were intimately involved with the developments in France and adopted as anti-Christian stances as many of the French revolutionaries themselves. If the appelation *founding fathers* refers to these men, we could hardly wish to pattern a modern-day revival of Christianity on their model. Paine boasted, "My own mind is my church," and Franklin insisted on a public religion that would promote morality and citizenship without meddling in affairs strictly reserved to the realm of reason (e.g., science or politics). This reads like Voltaire's creed: "The only book that should be read is the great book of nature. The sole religion is to worship God and to be an honorable man. This pure and everlasting religion cannot possibly produce harm."[18]

The Enlightenment views, which began to gain a following among the colonies' opinion leaders by the mid-eighteenth century, was later capsulated in William Ernest Henley's poem "Invictus":

> I thank whatever gods that be
>   for my unconquerable soul. . . .
> I am the master of my fate,
>   the captain of my soul.

Arminianism made the first tear in the fabric of evangelical orthodoxy, challenging the Reformation's insistence on the moral and spiritual inability of humans. At a time when liberty from sovereigns was the American goal, Arminianism became an ally of the civil religion of Jefferson and Franklin. A former professor of history at the University of Chicago, William Warren Sweet, observes:

> Arminianism became the theology of the common man because it jibed with his experience. As a practical man, he disliked 'dogmatic [doctrinal] subtlety and philosophical abstraction.' From the middle of the eighteenth century onward a whole series of revolts against Calvinism were in the making in America. . . . The first was the gradual rise of a social caste, especially in and around Boston, composed of families made up chiefly of prosperous merchants and professional men to whom the stern doctrines of Calvin had become increasingly repugnant. Their success in achieving wealth . . . easily convinced them that they were the masters of their own fates. . . . [19]

This was true not only for the Bostonian elite, but for the frontiersmen as well. Writes Sweet, "The Calvinistic idea that man had nothing to do with his own salvation made little sense to the frontiersman, who knew only too well that his temporal salvation was in his own hands." Calvinistic missionaries would "report that a whole region was destitute of religion, even though numerous other religious bodies were active in the territories."[20]

One could scarcely distinguish an Arminian and a deistic sermon. Franklin's "God helps those who help themselves" could have been seen on a church marquee in any number of places during the period leading up to the Revolutionary War. Indeed, the enduring significance of that comparison is demonstrated in the fact that many, even Christians, today believe Franklin's slogan to be a biblical quotation.

Especially with the Enlightenment, but even without it, Arminianism was suited to the new American temper. It was democratic in terms of the creature-Creator relationship; it offered a Ruler whom the free citizen elected instead of the dictatorship of a God who elected his citizens. In the former religion, one decided whether he would be a subject; in the latter, everyone was a subject, whether he accepted the Sovereign's lordship or not.

Secularist philosopher Michael Harrington notes, "At the same time that the Enlightenment put humans in God's traditional place at the center of the universe, it defined that universe as amoral."[21] Friedrich Nietzsche, a late-nine-teenth-century German philosopher, noted that in the wake of the Enlightenment, there were "signs of a complete uprooting of culture." "The waters of religion," he said, "are receding, leaving behind swamps and stagnant pools; nations are again dividing into opposite camps with the aim of destroying one another. . . . Never before was the world more worldly, and never was it poorer in love and goodness."[22] Voltaire had predicted that with the Enlightenment, dogmatism, wars of religion, and intolerance would be wiped out by rationalism. Unlike early Puritanism, with its balance between reason and revelation, the Enlightenment not only failed to provide ultimate answers; it left despair over whether there could be any.

The Great Awakening

Just when the Enlightenment began to gain converts, New England was awakened . . . for a time.

William Tennent, an Irish Presbyterian immigrant, and Theodore Frelinghuysen, a Dutch Reformed immigrant, both served parishes in New Jersey. In the 1720s, Frelinghuysen began to remind his own parishioners what Reformed Christians believed; Tennent, with his son Gilbert, began preaching the doctrines of grace widely. Disturbed by the spread of Arminianism, William Tennent founded the Log College in 1736. The little academy became a center for the Calvinistic evangelists and in 1746, the year of William Tennent's death, the Log College became the College of New Jersey, known to us as Princeton.

Meanwhile, Jonathan Edwards, born in 1703, tiptoed onto the scene. Shy and reserved, this grandson of Solomon Stoddard (the minister who initiated the Half-Way Covenant) was also eminently educated. According to the *Encyclopaedia Britannica*, Edwards is the keenest scholar America ever produced. At thirteen, he entered Yale; eventually he began a prolific career as a defender of the faith, with polemics on original sin, justification, and the freedom of the will. Unafraid of borrowing from the new science of John Locke and Isaac Newton, Edwards collected an impressive argument for the older New England orthodoxy.

In 1731, Edwards preached about "God Glorified in Man's Dependence" to the increasingly liberal establishment in Boston. The sermon title was calculated for his audience.

In 1735, revival broke out in his pastorate. Imagine, the greatest spiritual awakening this nation has ever known came as a result of preaching doctrine! Once indifferent to religion, entire towns became filled with discussions about God and salvation. Edwards recorded, "And wherever God's sovereignty with regard to the salvation of sinners was preached, there with it God sent revival." Exiled by a congregation that did not appreciate his message, in 1757 he accepted the presidency of Princeton, but died soon afterward. He was called "the last Puritan."

George Whitefield, an Anglican evangelist, took over where Edwards had left off. In fact, it was through Whitefield that the Great Awakening became a colonial, not merely a New England, phenomenon. According to Hofstadter, "As preachers it is doubtful that even such sterling nineteenth-century Americans as Charles Finney and Dwight L. Moody matched Whitefield, and none of the later platform clowns of the evangelical tradition, such as Billy Sunday, would bear comparison."[23] Franklin came to hear Whitefield and resolved not to give one penny to his orphanage; by the end of the sermon, the Philadelphia leader had emptied his pockets. He measured the span of the audience and concluded that Whitefield could be heard by thirty thousand, and also remarked, "From being thoughtless or indifferent about religion, it seemed as if all the world were growing religious, so that one could not walk through the town in an evening without hearing psalms sung in different families of every street."[24]

At Oxford, Whitefield had discovered the club founded by John and Charles Wesley. Though he was a Calvinist, Whitefield had a charitable attitude toward a variety of denominations. "Don't tell me you are a Baptist, an Independent, a Presbyterian, a dissenter, tell me you are a Christian, that is all I want," he said.[25]

Nevertheless, his friend and associate, John Wesley, published a tract titled "Free Grace," essentially a declaration of war on Calvinism. Devastated that Wesley would intentionally make the stand both knew would lead to a break in fellowship, Whitefield responded with his tract, "Why I Preach Electing Grace," and Wesley countered by founding the *Arminian Monthly*. Gerald R. Cragg observes, "To Whitefield it was clear that Arminianism dulled the all-important sense of sin; it made men complacent, whereas election tended to 'rouse the soul out of its carnal security. Was Wesley right, he asked, in holding that Calvinism killed all hope and led to indifference? Did not the contrary view surrender the vital concept of an almighty God? In his blunt way Wesley once told his friend [Whitefield] that 'your God is my devil.'"[26]

Whitefield was the most numerically successful evangelist to that date since the apostolic era. His clear appeals to the evangelical substance of the faith demonstrates for us still today, as do those of Edwards and the Tennents, that it is possible to have an educated mind and a warm heart, and that both are the only goal worthy of Christian piety. At least for a time, Calvinism survived at the center of American life.

Unwilling to accept a civil religion, Gilbert Tennent followed in his father's footsteps as a revivalist. "Repeatedly," writes Hofstadter, "the revivalists emphasized justification by faith and the experience of conversion, discounting the efficacy of good works and an upright life."[27] Charged with antinomianism (amoralism) by the Arminian establishment, the revivalists of the Great Awakening differed from the moralistic and anti-intellectual aspects that were to mark much of evangelicalism from the Second Awakening to the present.

The Great Awakening never won for Calvinism its former regency over the New England establishment. As the Awakening began to disintegrate into emotionalism and lost both the Reformed character as well as the intellectual framework of Edwards, Whitefield, and the Tennents, America was looking for a creed compatible with a Jacksonian democracy. According to the Pulitzer Prize–winning Harvard historian, Arthur Schlesinger, Jr., "By the time the revolutionaries came to Philadelphia in 1776, the flames of Calvinism were burning low. . . . Original sin, not yet abandoned, was, like everything else, secularized."[28]

The Growth of Evangelicalism

By the Revolutionary War, the cultural war between self-confident rationalism and self-confident emotionalism had already been waged. In the deistic religion of Boston Unitarians, Arminianism took on a rationalistic flavor, but in the enthusiastic, emotional, even radical temper of the frontier, Arminianism eventually became characterized by an antirationalistic spirit. In the former, people were taught to trust their reason, and in the latter, their emotions, but in both the individual was enshrined.

Hofstadter offers his insight on this point:

> The Puritan ideal of the minister as an intellectual and educational leader was steadily weakened in the face of the evangelical ideal of the minister as a popular . . . exhorter. Theological education itself became more instrumental.

Simple dogmatic formulations were considered sufficient. The churches withdrew from intellectual encounters with the secular world, gave up the idea that religion is a part of the whole life of intellectual experience, and often abandoned the field of rational studies on the assumption that they were the natural province of science alone.

By 1853 an outstanding clergyman complained that there was "an impression, somewhat general, that an intellectual clergyman is deficient in piety, and that an eminently pious minister is deficient in intellect."[29]

By the time of the Second Awakening (beginning in the last quarter of the eighteenth century through first quarter of the nineteenth), the existential act of faith replaced the objective content of faith in popular revivals. People wanted to decide for themselves which church came closest to their views. Sects proliferated. "The idea of a historical continuity in the life of the Church," says Hofstadter, "carries no weight whatever for the sect consciousness." In fact, "since there need be only a shadow of confessional unity in the denominations, the rational discussion of theological issues—in the past a great source of intellectual discipline in the churches—came to be regarded as a distraction, as a divisive force."[30] One alarm was reported in the *South Carolina Gazette* in 1741: The trained clergy, whether of the urbane Unitarian type, or of the orthodox variety, were being overthrown by "private persons of no education and but low attainment in knowledge and in the great doctrines of the Gospel."

By undermining the doctrinal, intellectual foundation of the faith, evangelicals left evangelicalism without a serious defense in that marketplace of ideas it once built, but from which it was now evicted. By default, secularism became an inevitable force shaping American public and private life. "But how is such a separate self to be shaped and grounded?" ask Robert N. Bellah and his co-authors in *Habits of the Heart*. "Do we have answers today that correspond to those provided by Winthrop's God . . . ?"[31] We had indeed gone the way of Eve, but were we enlightened? "Today religion in America," according to Bellah, "is as private and diverse as New England colonial religion was public and unified."[32]

America at its founding was anything but a Christian nation.The founding fathers accepted a civil, not a supernatural, religious perspective that falls far short of biblical Christianity. By 1790, 90 percent of the American population was unchurched. Even in their present state of secularization, modern France and Great Britain have double the church attendance of post-Revolutionary America.[33] Further, in secularized modern America, church or synagogue attendance is ranked at 40 percent weekly.[34]

Contemporary Reverberations

Although some of the causes of secularism may be explained in terms of the distractions of urbanization and technology, most can be located in the collapse of the profound vision of Christianity that was recaptured by the Reformation. Early in our past we broke with the confessional orthodoxy that had given us a place to stand, explaining all of life in a unified, meaningful way. As our knowledge and raw data accumulated rapidly, so our ability to arrange the information in a theocentric picture faded.

The new American needed a sense of autonomy. John T. McNeill wrote, "Most Calvinists have always associated with their faith in the sovereignty of God a feeling for the cause of human liberty and public justice and a strong preference for representative and responsible government."[35] In Scotland, John Knox defied Mary Stuart and built Presbyterianism on a representative government. Out of this faith Samuel Rutherford, who participated in the drafting of the Westminster Confession of Faith, wrote his celebrated *Lex Rex*, arguing that the ruler derived his authority from the people. Rutherford's arguments were widely employed dur could be cited in other lands: in Holland's liberation from Spain; the Protestant struggle in France, Switzerland, and parts of Germany, Hungary, and Poland. The English Civil War, led by Cromwell and the Calvinist-dominated parliament, ended absolute monarchy in Britain. "Cromwell," notes one source, "was a devoted Puritan who desired religious toleration, a godly nation, and a representative government."[36]

The point is that democracy is not only consistent with, but also a natural product of, the Reformed tradition in early colonial history. And yet, as democratic as that tradition might be on the horizontal level (creature to creature), it is autocratic on the vertical level (Creator to creature). As the Scottish minister in *Chariots of Fire* corrected his more liberally-minded auditor, "God is not running a democracy, but a dictatorship." A government "of the people, for the people, and by the people" was conceived with Christian aid, but it is impossible to ignore the fact that a religion "of the people, for the people, and by the people" came to dominate the vertical (creature-Creator) relationship as well. This, of course, is disastrous for a religion in which God, not the individual, reigns. "For from him and through him and to him are all things. To him be the glory forever! Amen." (Rom. 11:36). "In short," argue historians Mark A. Noll, Nathan Hatch, and George Marsden, "Calvinism was being dropped not in response to theological arguments but because it violated the spirit of Revolutionary liberty."[37]

The "Consistent Calvinists," the students of the Great Awakening, planted the seeds of the Second Awakening. In addition to personal conversion, there was a renewed stress on public justice. The women's suffrage movement and the abolition of slavery were championed by these students of Edwards and Tennent. Even when the later revivalists abandoned the theological framework motivating these public reforms, they carried on the tradition of uniting personal faith and social well-being. It was not until the pessimism of the First World War overcame the triumphalistic postmillenialism of the previous two-and-a-half centuries that evangelicals finally divorced their personal faith from worldly affairs.

As we gave away more territory, *we* secularized America.

It was we who left a vacuum to be filled by alternative world views. Unbelief grows because the reasons for faith are either internally inadequate or because they are inadequately defended. It is easy to lay the responsibility on secular humanists, but it is not quite honest. And honesty is essential in an hour such as ours. We ourselves left the neighborhood of ideas and retreated into our own private ghetto, where evangelical religion has been aptly, though tragically, characterized as privately engaging, but socially irrelevant. Cox put it this way: "Secularism . . . has relativized religious world views and thus rendered them innocuous. Religion has been privatized. . . . Secularization has accomplished what fire and chain could not: it has convinced the believer that he *could* be wrong, and persuaded the devotee that there are more important things than dying for the faith. The gods of traditional religions live on as private fetishes or the patrons of congenial groups, but they play no role whatever in the public life of the secular metropolis."[38]

Since Christians themselves have privatized their faith, the societal station wagon has been forced to seek alternative fuel: it runs on the fumes of quasi-Christian gasoline. There is no such thing as a value-free culture, anymore than there can be a color-free green. To attack the world for being worldly is not only poor manners, but also a profound waste of time. As Ernst Renan, the French philosopher who lost his faith in seminary, wrote, "We are living on the perfume of an empty vase."[39] But we still have the recipe! What is needed now is not calls to those for whom the gospel is still "foolishness" to comply with a civil religion, to take another whiff of the empty vase, but to fill the vase again with its ancient essence.

To do this, we ourselves will have to learn the ingredients again, taking nothing for granted—as though we, like the Philippian jailer, were asking, "What must I do to be saved?" (Acts 16:30). Calvinism has offered one answer to that question, an answer it considers the biblical one. While the Reformed interpretation cannot be judged true on the basis of tradition, it cannot be judged false on that basis. "Our culture's indifference to the past," writes Christopher Lasch in his best-selling book, *The Culture of Narcissism*, "furnishes the most telling proof of that culture's bankruptcy."[40]

Whether one embraces a Calvinistic, Arminian, Unitarian, or secular world view, the shift from the first to the following systems was central in the process of secularization. A noted historian, Joseph Haroutunian, remarks:

> Before, religion was God-centered. Before, whatever was not conducive to the glory of God was infinitely evil; now that which is not conducive to the happiness of man is evil, unjust, and impossible to attribute to the deity. Before, the good of man consisted ultimately in glorifying God; now the glory of God consists in the good of man. Before, man lived to glorify God; now God lived to serve man.[41]

Jerry Falwell tells us we need to "come back to the faith of our fathers, to the Bible of our fathers, and to the biblical principles that our fathers used as a premise for this nation's establishment."[42] However, the evidence seems to suggest that the "faith of our founding fathers" was not a biblical faith, but a mixture of Enlightenment deism, Arminianism, and secularized traces of the older biblical faith. (For example, John Adams spoke freely about "this awful blasphemy" of the deity of Christ.)

Furthermore, one can even contest turning to the "Bible of our fathers" if by that one means the bible of Jefferson, applauded by Franklin, Paine, Ethan Allen, and John Adams. In this revised bible, Jefferson had expunged the supernatural elements (the miracles, the deity of Christ, the virgin birth, and the resurrection) and other teachings considered offensive to the rationalistic and self-determinative sensitivities of the new American. John Adams's attitude toward the Bible is characteristic: "It contains more of my little Phylosophy than all of the Libraries I have seen: and such Parts of it as I cannot reconcile to my little Phylosophy I postpone for future Investigation." That sort of a view of

Christianity's central authority might be acceptable for a broadly based, syncretistic civil religion, but it is an archenemy of genuine faith. It might help us secure plastic nativity scenes on the lawn of the county courthouse, but it will only hinder the cause of Christ by confusing the gospel with an establishment of an essentially deistic religion.

Finally, a great many of the "principles that our fathers used as a premise for this nation's establishment" were far from Christian in the biblical sense. During the mid-eighteenth century, "church members never amounted to more than a third of the population of New England adults and may never have been as high as five percent of adults in the southern colonies."[43] No less a founding father than George Washington proclaimed in a letter to Tripoli, "As the government of the United States of America is not in any sense founded on the Christian Religion, . . . it is declared by the parties that no pretext arising from religious opinions shall ever produce an interruption of the harmony existing between the two countries."[44]

Folk religion is not better than no religion at all. It is dangerous to confuse biblical Christianity with paganism. We are part of an increasingly pluralistic society and we cannot expect unbelievers to superficially embrace an outward "form of godliness but deny its power" (2 Tim. 3:5). We must enter the public square as missionaries sent to a new field where Christ is not known, where eight in ten Americans say they are Christians, but only four in ten know Jesus delivered the Sermon on the Mount and fewer than half can name the four Gospels.[45]

"Puritanism in its flowering time was a revolution," writes Yale historian Sydney Ahlstrom. "Evangelicalism is a counter-revolution; it does not joyfully reap the harvest of the Puritan quadricentennium and then turn those riches to solutions for the frightening problems . . . of the post-Puritan world." Instead, it condemns the world for being worldly while offering no compelling, intelligent alternative. "This," says Ahlstrom, "may be a very risky strategy.

And one may doubt that it is the best way to convey the riches of a great tradition to a needy world."[46]

"The consequence," according to Haroutunian, "was a theology which succeeded merely in becoming a 'legalistic' and 'dialectical' superstructure in a practically alien world." And yet, he adds a note of hope: "It is probable that a revival of the 'tragic sense of life,' together with the wisdom and sobriety which grow out of it, should be forthcoming. It is necessary that men rediscover the truths once signified by the doctrines of divine sovereignty and divine grace, of predestination and election, of depravity and regeneration."[47] While these doctrines of classical Protestantism may not be polite, both their biblical origin and their historic significance cannot be denied.

Let us conclude with a warning by United States Senator Mark Hatfield:

> Many believe that civil religion is better than no religion at all. But I wonder. Civil religion, in my view, is not a harmless, generalized unitarianlike depository of belief, which can help people reflect on God, or even provide helpful ethical guides for the country. Rather, because most civil religion is devoid of both the prophetic dimension of biblical faith and of the centrality of God's revelation in Jesus Christ, it becomes highly vulnerable to being exploited as a tool of national self-righteousness and even idolatry.
>
> We must not settle for imitations, no matter how harmless they may appear to be. When it comes to Christianity, in harmlessness is found the greatest harm.[48]

The "How To" Gospel 2

Perfection of means and confusion of ends seem to
characterize our age.
—Albert Einstein

I caught myself impatiently commanding my FAX
machine to hurry. It has come to that, hasn't it? We are cra-
dled by technology to the extent that a letter which used to
take a few days or a week to arrive can now arrive any-
where in the world in a matter of minutes. And yet, there I
was, tensely holding the paper taut between my fingers,
almost pulling it, in an effort to speed the already unfath-
omable technological achievement. No doubt there are
enough people like me who never seem to be happy with
such advances and always want more. Before long, the
marketplace will demand a new and improved replacement
for the marvel.

The technological revolution involves more than office
equipment and household appliances. There is a method or
technique for everything under the sun: "How to Build Your
Own Kitchen," "How to Become a Millionaire without Any

39

Talent, Money, or Energy," "How to Rear Perfect Children," "How to Have a Positive Mental Attitude," and so on. We gauge our tools, our beliefs, and even our lives by the standard of usefuless.

Education, according to Allan Bloom, has succumbed to the pressures of pragmatism, too. "Even the life of reason is often unappealing," he says, "and useless knowledge, [that is], knowledge that is not obviously useful for a career, has no place in the student's vision of the curriculum."[1] A cursory survey of the average university catalogue demonstrates that educational institutions have shifted from providing an integrated world view to serving as smorgasbords of diverse and unrelated opinions and trends.

Some years ago, I attended a course at the International Institute of Human Rights in Strasbourg, France. In one session held at the European Parliament, the gentleman in charge of the parliament's statement on genetic engineering addressed our group. After discussing some examples of ethical and human rights-related decisions Europeans are having to make in the light of recent technological advances, he observed the gap between our scientific, practical sophistication and our immature grasp of what to do with it all. "We're technological giants," he said with his heavy French accent, "but moral and intellectual dwarves."

In *Habits of the Heart,* the authors paraphrase Eva Brann's *Paradoxes of Education in a Republic*: "She argues that in education at present, the choice is either tradition or technique, and that technique has become far too dominant. . . . When education becomes an instrument for individual careerism, it cannot provide either personal meaning or civic culture."[2]

Now take the cautions these educators have issued for their discipline and apply them to contemporary Christianity, replacing the word *education* with "the church." Bloom's comment translates, "Even the life of *faith and* reason *(thinking through one's faith and its relationship to daily life)* is often unappealing and useless knowledge *(or doctrine),* that is, knowledge that is not obviously useful to *'the Christian walk'* has no place in the *believer's* vision of the *Christian life.*"

The paraphrase from Eva Brann translates, "In *Christianity* at present, the choice is either tradition or technique, and that technique has become far too dominant. . . . When *the Bible* becomes an instrument for individual *rules and steps to this or that*, it cannot provide either personal meaning or *Christian community*."

The Evangelical Roots of Pragmatism

As we will see, it is almost as true that America is made in the church as it is that the church is made in America. In many ways, evangelicalism helped create the pragmatic elements in modern secular culture. Richard Hofstadter notes, "Anything that seriously diminished the role of rationality and learning in early American religion would later diminish its role in secular culture. The feeling that ideas should above all be made to work, the disdain for doctrine and for refinements in ideas, the subordination of men of ideas to men of emotional power or manipulative skill are hardly innovations of the twentieth century; they are inheritances from American Protestantism."[3]

Where does Hofstadter get this notion of American evangelicalism embracing a pragmatic creed even before its official adoption by the larger culture? One can contrast the Great Awakening (mid-eighteenth century), led by George Whitefield and Jonathan Edwards, with the Second Awakening (early nineteenth century). In the initial Awakening, Edwards, a theological, philosophical, and scientific genius is also an evangelist. He calls people to faith in Christ on the basis of clear proclamation of doctrines—even the unpopular ones of original sin, justification, and the sovereignty of God. Whitefield finds ways of working election and other major doctrines into his evangelistic sermons. And yet, the movement sweeps the colonies into an unprecedented revival.

In the Second Awakening, however, the message shifts from God to man. In the first Awakening, the emphasis is on what God has done; in the Second, on what man can and must do. Thus, a whole system of techniques and methods emerges in order to assist (some said manipulate) audiences into doing what they must do in order to achieve salvation. For Edwards and Whitefield, a revival is the sovereign act of God's Spirit; for Nathaniel Taylor and Charles Finney, it is "nothing more than the right use of means."[4]

According to a University of California professor, Stephen Berk, the New England Calvinists "had to adjust their theology to a more secular climate." New Divinity men like Timothy Dwight "met the challenge by discarding the supernaturalism of the Great Awakening and formulating a revised practical Calvinism." The result was that the Second Awakening, "unlike the earlier one, . . . was not a spontaneous upwelling of faith, but a calculated endeavor, planned and executed by conservative evangelicals. As the acknowledged leader of this Protestant Counter-Reformation, Dwight did much to set its tone and pace."[5] Those seeking a single movement responsible for the character of contemporary evangelicalism need look no further than the Second Awakening. Here, Berk concurs, "the fusion of evangelical Protestantism with American cultural values really began to take shape."[6]

As we learned in the previous chapter, the shift from the Great Awakening to the Second and from the Reformation faith of the early Puritans to the deism of the founding fathers is in many ways a shift from Calvinism to Arminianism. Says Berk, "If consistent Calvinism was the most supernaturalist position among 18th-century Puritans, Arminianism was the most man-centered." While the Calvinists proclaimed the absolute dependence of the sinner on God's grace, "Arminians preached a more self-reliant and moralistic theology."[7]

George Marsden notes, "After Edwards' time revivalist theology in America moved steadily toward emphasizing the human side of religious experience. . . . Free will was virtually an American dogma."[8] Especially in the Jacksonian democracy, salvation now was "of the people, for the people, and by the people," and conversion depended on finding and using the right methods. Evangelistic technique began to overshadow interest in the content of the gospel being preached.

The generation of theologians, particularly at Yale, which produced the Second Awakening, insisted that they were Calvinists and that they held firmly to the convictions of irresistible grace, justification, election, and the rest. And yet, Bellamy, for instance, "subordinated doctrine to practice," Berk writes. In theory, Bellamy agreed that God's regenerating grace "must be irresistible and supernatural." But in practice, he urged his audiences to "look diligently lest you fail the grace of God by resisting the Holy Spirit." Berk adds, "Earlier in the same sermon, he had exhorted sinners to consider their most pressing self-interest. Religious devotions were a matter of utmost 'expediency' and would be of inestimable personal 'advantage.' These arguments appealed to the very attributes of self-love that Bellamy and all consistent Calvinists decried as evil in God's sight." Thus, "Bellamy, in his evangelistic fervor, had violated the principle of divine sovereignty and sacrificed holy love on the altar of utility."[9]

This is an important development. In the Great Awakening, Reformed theology was not only *not* a noose around an evangelist's neck; it was the necessary substance and motivation for genuine revival. In the Second Awakening, there is an emerging dichotomy between what a Yale professor holds in his creed and what he proclaims on the evangelistic stage. Eventually, the utility of a man-centered message in a man-centered Jacksonian democracy overwhelmed even the theoretical adherence to Reformed theology.

For instance, Timothy Dwight, Edwards's grandson, came to deny that justification—that truth by which, according to the Reformers, the church stands or falls—is an objective, legal declaration of righteousness, but taught instead that it is a subjective, inward transformation of the heart and life. This, of course, was the position of the Roman Catholic

Church in its condemnation of Protestantism. Dwight concluded that he could no longer be convinced that the believer's righteousness is Christ's alone, that nothing the believer did could affect that justification.

But now, it would not be the professors who would take theology (whether good or bad theology) to the evangelistic crusades. It would be those brave souls on horseback who would take the new evangelical confidence in human ability to the frontiers.

The circuit riders who traversed the Appalachians under adverse conditions frequently represented the thinking of the rugged individualists with whom they came into contact. According to Hofstadter, "They evolved a kind of crude pietistic pragmatism with a single essential tenet: their business was to save souls as quickly and as widely as possible. For this purpose, the elaborate theological equipment of an educated ministry was not only an unnecessary frill but in all probability a serious handicap; the only justification needed by the itinerant preacher for his limited stock of knowledge and ideas was that he got results, measurable in conversions. To this justification very little answer was possible."[10]

The gulf between the truth-centered evangelism of Edwards and Whitefield and the technique-centered variety of industrialized religion is illustrated by Charles Finney (1792–1875), whose *Systematic Theology* was hailed for its usefulness. "Many servants of our Lord," the foreword of a modern edition reads, "should be diligently searching for a gospel that 'works,' and I am happy to state they can find it in this volume."[11]

Finney himself said that sinners are "required to effect" regeneration. "The sinner," he wrote, "has all the faculties and natural attributes requisite to render perfect obedience to God. All he needs is to be induced."[12] Hence, for Finney, both conversion and the process of sanctification depended not on divine grace, but on human technique. Said Finney, "A revival is not a miracle, or dependent on a miracle in any sense. It is a purely philosophic result of the right use of means."[13]

Toward the end of the nineteenth century, revivalism was led by Dwight L. Moody. As Moody put it, "It makes no difference how you get a man to God, provided you get him there."[14] Marsden observes, "Moody judged his sermons . . . by whether they were 'fit to convert sinners with.'"[15]

After Moody, a baseball player turned evangelist, Billy Sunday, burst onto the scene, stirring audiences by his dramatic performances on the evangelistic stage. When the press asked him why he had become wealthy through the revivals, the evangelist retorted, "What I'm paid for my work makes it only about $2 a soul, and I get less proportionately for the number I convert than any other living evangelist."[16] Sunday also said, "I believe there is no doctrine more dangerous than to convey the impression that a revival is something peculiar in itself and cannot be judged by the same rules of causes and effect as other things."[17] As Martin E. Marty remarks, "The preaching of revival was designed to accent what a person had to achieve all alone, almost by an act of will."[18]

This represents a tremendous irony in Christian history. After all, Christianity has always been a supernatural religion. To the Galatians, Saint Paul issued severe warnings about beginning with a strong confidence in God's grace and then gradually giving in to that all-too-human temptation to trust self-will and self-effort. "I am astonished," he penned, "that you are so quickly deserting the one who called you by the grace of Christ and are turning to a different gospel—which is really no gospel at all" (Gal. 1:6–7). "You foolish Galatians! Who has bewitched you? . . . Are you so foolish? After beginning with the Spirit, are you now trying to attain your goal by human effort?" (3:1, 3).

Thus, the irony of evangelical pragmatism in the tradition of Taylor, Finney, Moody, and Sunday is particularly obvious for a faith that is intrinsically opposed to this sort of thinking about God and salvation. When we recall the tempest caused by Sunday and his fellow revivalists over the prejudices against supernaturalism in modern thinking, the irony is highlighted. After all, if salvation, the most sacred matter of divine activity, is stripped of its supernaturalism and reduced to technique, why should biology fit supernatural explanations?

Even hyper-supernaturalism becomes naturalistic at the hands of pragmatism. For instance, today's faith healers tell us that our faith is the finger which flips the switch of cosmic power. If we follow the prescribed formula (e.g., hand on the screen, financial contribution, repetition of a prayer, application of a prayer cloth), God's healing power is guaranteed to operate in response. Pat Robertson urges Christians to employ the "laws of prosperity," to which God himself is bound. "It's a bit like tuning into a radio or television station," he writes. "You get on the right frequency and you pick up the program."[19] And what are we to say of those who are never healed or who never get that financial miracle? "He has either failed to grasp the points we have been making . . . about the operation of the kingdom or is not living according to the major principles we have been exploring."[20] God's sovereignty used to comfort people in their distress, as they took heart in knowing "all things work together for good." But for many in today's pragmatic self-help religion, God's mysterious will is replaced with the believer's failure to employ the correct principles, techniques, and methods which manipulate God and the universe.

While there is a great deal of mysticism among modern faith healers, they actually eliminate mystery from miracle, making healing predictable and, in fact, inevitable (naturalistic). No longer is a miracle the spontaneous and surprising work of God, but the right use of means, as predictable as any other scientific law. When God heals, it is not an interruption of natural laws. At its core, the faith healers proclaim a naturalistic faith. Salvation and healing are both human achievements. What we need to see is the incongruity between having a religion that accents the rhetoric of miracle, but actually eliminates the miraculous from salvation and even from healing itself.

The Secular Roots of Modern Pragmatism

John Stuart Mill (1806–1873) exercised tremendous influence over American thought and, at his hand, the tendency to pragmatism which lay deep in the American frontier character and which shaped evangelists like Taylor and Finney now became a philosophical system.

John Dewey (1859–1952) carried pragmatism into a wider circle, making its presence felt especially in education, where it was suggested that the purpose of education is utility rather than the knowledge of a specific body of ideas, values, and facts. What works for one person does not necessarily work for another. Therefore, the goal of education is not to nurture people's intellects so that the result is an enlightened society, but to give individuals a chance to realize their full potential. As many modern educators decry the havoc Dewey's pragmatism has wreaked on education, so too we ought to recognize the ways in which pragmatism has shaped the evangelical mind.

But of all the pragmatists, no one had so much to do with the all-pervasive influence of that way of thinking than William James (1842–1910). Son of a theologian, James taught physiology, psychology, and philosophy at Harvard from 1872 to 1907. Though he was its chief systematizer, the Industrial Revolution would have raised pragmatic thought to dominance with or without the Harvard philosopher. No philosophy department was a match for the industrial and technological revolution sweeping Western nations. The fastest, least expensive way of getting things done now ruled the marketplace. As quantity began to compete with quality and volume threatened to displace craftsmanship, the towering spires of cathedrals pointing heavenward were overshadowed by towering office buildings designed to accommodate executives who sought increased efficiency and practicality. The contrast in outlooks could even be seen in the architecture. Efficiency, not aesthetics, was the chief concern, and these skyscrapers were staggering icons worthy of a new kind of veneration by those who served at their altars.

In *Pragmatism,* James devotes one chapter to the implications of his philosophy on religion. Why should we believe in God? In the past, this question has evoked a variety of answers, ranging from Anselm's ontological argument to Thomas Aquinas's five proofs to more modern theories. But never before had divine existence been posited on purely pragmatic grounds: "On pragmatistic principles, if the hypothesis of God *works satisfactorily* in the widest sense of the word, it is true" (italics added). "You see," James wrote, "pragmatism has to postpone dogmatic answer, for we do not yet know certainly which type of religion is going to work best in the long run." Thus, the value of knowing a particular truth depends on "the truth's cash-value in experiential terms."[21]

It is not difficult to notice how thoroughly this outlook has permeated modern thinking in general and Christian thinking in particular. We assess the worth of knowing this doctrine or that theological position on the basis of its usefulness or "cash-value in experiential terms," quite apart from viewing growth "in the grace and knowledge of our Lord and Savior Jesus Christ" (2 Pet. 3:18) as an end in itself. Rather than seeing Christ merely a power source or a teacher of practical principles, the Bible reveals Christ as the One "in whom are hidden all the treasures of wisdom and knowledge" (Col. 2:3). But, more importantly, it reveals him as the sacrifice for sins. This brings up our final consideration, as we seek to put both the evangelical and the secular roots of pragmatism to the test of Scripture.

Is Christianity Practical?

In *The Magician's Nephew,* C. S. Lewis writes, "Now that she was left alone with the children, she took no notice of either of them. And that was like her too. In Charn she had taken no notice of Polly (till the very end) because Digory was the one she wanted to make use of. Now that she had Uncle Andrew, she took no notice of Digory. I expect most witches are like that. They are not interested in things or people unless they can use them; they are terribly practical." This sounds all too familiar when we think of how we view our relationship with God and others. We are all incredibly utilitarian. But that is only because we are, at root, selfish. For James, the verification of God's existence is his usefulness. Like a new bug spray, God has to pass the test of utility for admission into the marketplace. How does God help me get what I want quickly, efficiently, easily, and with minimal cost? Furthermore, James tells us, religion can get along with pragmatism, just as long as religion doesn't make dogmatic assertions. "For we do not know what will work best in the long run."

Somewhere we must have agreed to the arrangement. I grew up with the familiar refrain, "It works for me," as a justification for belief. Testimonies were designed to show us how Christianity worked for a person. Once the person asked Jesus into his or her heart, problems suddenly vanished. But what do you do when Mormons and other cultists claim the same "testimonies"? Marriages put back together again, alcoholics turned into upstanding citizens, financial ruin turned around—what self-help group or religious sect cannot point to practical triumphs?

I even remember the preacher regularly telling us just before the invitation to accept Christ, "You know, even if Christianity is the biggest lie ever told, have you lost anything by following Jesus? Hasn't your life been improved?" I've always thought that an odd apologetic in the light of Saint Paul's charge that "if only for this life we have hope in Christ, we are to be pitied more than all men" (1 Cor. 15:19). The New Testament views the success of Christianity in the objective truth of that historical event of Christ's death for our sins and his being raised for our justification, not in its usefulness for living a jollier and fuller life.

According to the pragmatic interpretation of evangelical faith, Christianity has to compete with other self-help programs. It has to promise health, wealth, and happiness. But what happens when something works better? What happens when, like Digory in Lewis's story, Christianity outlives its usefulness? What happens when my wife and I become Christians and our marriage falls apart anyway? If Radio Shack can offer a product that can, as they advertise, "put the whole world in your hand," is Christianity all that practical by comparison?

Does Christianity work? That depends on what one conceives the problem to be. If our most immediate problem is a new car, the healing of a physical ailment, or "winning friends and influencing people," then Christianity will not be practical. For the car, the best thing might be a loan from the bank; for healing, a visit to a doctor; and for popularity there may be more practical remedies than Christianity. I am not saying that our faith has nothing to say about these things. But when we use the Bible as an answer book for the questions it does not consider important, we not only miss out on God's best answers; we end up despairing of the Bible's usefulness altogether. In other words, we have to go to the Bible not only for answers, but for questions. We need to find out what the most important—indeed, the most practical—issues really are.

The problem the Bible tackles is this: 'There is no one righteous, not even one; there is no one who understands, no one who seeks God. All have turned away, they have together become worthless; there is no one who does good, not even one'. . . . For all have sinned and fall short of the glory of God. . . . For the wages of sin is death" (Rom. 3:10–12, 23; 6:23). That's the problem as God sees it. It may not deal with the kind of problems we usually think about. But once the issue is raised, we usually recognize it for what it is. That is what needs to happen. We need to go back to the Scriptures for the questions as well as the answers. We must stop trivializing the Scriptures by pretending that they address practical themes with which they are not all that concerned.

In many ways, Christianity doesn't work. It has ruined some crafty businessmen like Zacchaeus, who, by becoming a Christian, ended up giving half his estate to the poor and paying back those he had cheated four times the amount he had stolen.

It is this God in whom a woman, Joni Eareckson Tada, placed her trust even though he had included in his mysterious plan a swimming accident that would leave her paralyzed. Without that tragedy, the contemporary Christian witness would be poorer. Not only did God not cancel the accident; he did not heal her, even after she sought healing earnestly. (Of course, Christianity is practical ultimately, even in this sense, in the hope of resurrection.)

His faith cost Dietrich Bonhoeffer his life when he opposed Hitler. In *The Cost of Discipleship*, Bonhoeffer wrote, "When Christ calls a man, He bids him come and die." That's a religion that doesn't work, from the secular, self-centered viewpoint.

I'm not even sure that Christianity works if the goal is happiness. There are deeply satisfying feelings I have of being secure, at peace, close to God. But there are also deeply troubling feelings. There are deeply disturbing times of wrestling with a God who reveals himself as someone other than the God I would like to worship. And there are times when the gospel's implications force me to enter a period of intense internal struggle. I remember hearing preachers say that non-Christians are unhappy and unfulfilled, while Christians are "victorious" and "happy in the Lord." But that isn't always true. I know non-Christians who are very happy. In fact, it is their contentedness which leads them to avoid discussions of religion. They don't think they need it.

If we seek to justify Christianity on pragmatic grounds, ours will continue to be just another self-help, self-improvement program. Among the array of wonder drugs and guaranteed formulas, Christianity may continue to be stocked, but only as long as it is not replaced by something that works better.

Temporal salvation, however, is not the goal of the gospel. The Bible doesn't offer us simple solutions to our political, financial, or physical ills. Many of us, I'm afraid, fall prey to the popular notion that even the most intricate political dilemmas have a simple solution presented in the form of a slogan or a Bible verse. For example, abortion is our generation's holocaust; nevertheless, do we on one hand condemn abortion and on the other encourage it by ignoring economic and societal factors which contribute dramatically to such an alternative? Or, can we be sure of how God feels about the occupied West Bank of Palestine? Can we assume that AIDS is merely God's judgment on homosexuals?

Oversimplification has afflicted our contemporaries and has left us with our own casualties. We turn to a doctor expecting a quick fix for our medical problems; we turn to a politician or party to fix moral ills; we turn to our mechanic for a quick fix of our automotive frustrations; and we turn to our preachers for a quick fix for our spiritual ills, often ignoring the deeper questions involved. So everything becomes "steps," "how to . . . ," and if someone protests that there is something more, something deeper, the cry is raised, "We want the practical!" Yet, we would do well to take to heart the caution of veteran journalist Edward R. Murrow: "Our major obligation is not to mistake slogans for solutions."

When Christ said, "If the Son sets you free, you will be free indeed," he had in mind something far more meaningful than financial, political, national, or physical freedom—as important as those aspects of our life are. Our Lord never promised a quick fix (this side of the resurrection) for anything beyond our reconciliation to God. "In this world," he assured his followers, "you will have trouble" (John 16:33). At last, a Savior who tells the truth! A Solution who doesn't make campaign promises we know he can't keep!

The Exploitation of the Faith

As we learned in chapter 1, the seed of civil religion (that is, a religion that worked best for society) was planted. Pragmatism is only a further, more systematic exploitation of vague Christianity. The eminent British research group, Oxford Analytica, predicts, "As American religion is exploited

for its functional usefulness, it will be vulnerable to deforma-
tion, involving a subtler change than the virtual collapse of
European religion" (italics added).[22]

We do need to be relevant. We must be able to demonstrate to our contemporaries that Christianity does not
ignore, but in fact faces, the most pressing problems of
modern times. But we trivialize our faith when it has to
match the evening news. We have a tendency to see the
immediate problems, whether personal or public, as ultimate, and we are amazed to see on the evening news a
report marking the one-year anniversary of an earthquake
or the ten-year anniversary of a truce. When those events
were in the headlines, we thought they were ultimate, but
a year has passed, ten years, and the world goes on.

In other ways Christianity is exploited for its usefulness.
If there is a biblical book which characterizes our evangelical churches today, it would be Proverbs. For the
Reformation and subsequent Protestantism, it was Romans.
Notice the difference in focus. Of course, Proverbs is a
canonical book and there is sound, practical advice there.
But look at the Epistle to the Romans, that magnificent systematic theology of the Bible. It is possible to meet a fellow
believer who uses the wisdom of Proverbs in planning his
financial portfolio, but who could not explain justification
to save his life. This, I think, is a preoccupation which ultimately trivializes and exploits the faith.

We must beware of confusing technique with truth. It is
assumed that there is a Christian way, method, or technique
for doing everything from jumping up and down to music
(Christian aerobics) to installing refrigerators (Christian busi-
nesses). When Christians think this way for very long, they
are bound to diminuate the wealth of biblical insight. The
next generation will see such faith as superficial and shallow
solutions for equally trivial problems.

Solving the Real Problems

Is Christianity, then, a problem-solving religion? Yes, if
one is talking about the problem God has with humanity.

On the cross, Christ abolished the enmity between God and his people. In Christ "there is now no condemnation" (Rom. 8:1). God's problem was that he loved people who hated him and wanted to be a Father to people to whom he, in his holiness and justice, could only relate as Judge. How could he save those he loved while maintaining his justice?

He couldn't merely overlook sin; that would deny his justice. And yet, "'there is no one righteous, not even one'" (Rom. 3:10). If "all have sinned" (Rom. 3:23), and "the wages of sin is death" (6:23), all must die. That is the real problem. Therefore, he devises a plan to sacrifice his own Son as a substitute for all believers, pouring out his wrath and just sentence on a sinless victim. In this marvelous exchange, our unrighteousness is nailed to the cross (Col. 2:13–15) and Christ's righteousness is imputed to our account. This justification before God is accepted by the believer by faith alone. "All this is from God, who reconciled us to himself through Christ and gave us the ministry of reconciliation: that God was reconciling the world to himself in Christ, not counting men's sins against them. . . . We implore you on Christ's behalf: Be reconciled to God. God made him who had no sin to be sin for us, so that in him we might become the righteousness of God" (2 Cor. 5:18–21).

The problem of death, a source of tremendous anxiety in our society, is answered. "'Death is swallowed up in victory. . . . Where, O death, is your sting?'" (1 Cor. 15:54, 55). No longer is death a threat, but a passage to the presence of God as we await the final resurrection, the reunion of body and soul in their original perfection.

These, and a host of other benefits of Christ's life, passion, and resurrection, solve our deepest problems—problems we would probably push into the background if the Bible didn't remind our consciences of their importance. Suddenly, the idea of what is practical changes drastically.

Although there are horizontal as well as vertical implications of Christian truth, Christianity is not concerned with safety pins and blenders, but with the safety of sinners in God's everlasting arms. Its themes surround the repair of broken relationships, starting with our relationship with God, not broken cars or appliances. It solves the most fundamental human problems, which are often ignored when Christians follow the world in asking the wrong, or at least peripheral, questions. Further, the world itself begins to distrust a church that does no more than mimic its own voice when the church claims to be speaking for God.

The "quick-fix Deity" doesn't exist. He is a fictional character, a piece of Americana. In a conversation, James Boice made this statement: "Christianity is not a way of going *around* human problems, but a way of going *through* them in a way that really honors God. And this," he added, "is the faith that overcomes the world."

Conclusion

A casual inventory of evangelical periodicals, tapes, and books reveals that there is little difference between the Christian's demand for a utilitarian faith and the non-Christian's never-ending search for a new fix. But if we are going to win our contemporaries, it will not be by trying to convince them that Christianity is more practical than, for example, New Age mysticism; it will not, in other words, be through demonstrating that the Christian faith answers the unbeliever's quest for something that works better than other self-improvement programs, but that Christianity starts with fundamentally different questions.

It must be reaffirmed, then, that conversion as well as Christian growth is the work of God for humans, not the work of humans for God. Pragmatic, man-centered evangelism must be replaced with a concern for relating the truth of the gospel to people. Technique-oriented evangelism is deficient for two reasons. First, it treats human beings as target audiences to be manipulated into conversion, not as creatures who bear God's image and who, being fallen, need a supernatural act of divine grace to make our proclamation effective. Method-centered approaches exploit human problems and often make promises they can't keep.

Even friendships with unbelievers become a technique instead of being genuine. Biblical evangelism is concerned with people, not programs.

Second, technique-centered evangelism is wrong because of the way it treats God like an absentee landlord. Essentially, pragmatic religion is deistic. While acknowledging God's existence, deism conceives a god who leaves the world to itself. It treats conversion in terms of "the right use of means" (Finney) rather than a supernatural intrusion of God. The pragmatic gospel asserts that as God provided a world and left its fate in the hands of its inhabitants, so God provided salvation and left its success or failure in the hands of efficient and clever evangelists. Perhaps indeed our faith does reflect the religion of our founding fathers, and tragically so. Strip Christianity of its supernaturalism, leaving only a skeleton of public morality—this was the benign religion envisioned by deism. Pragmatic evangelism reduces Christianity to just that.

In a series of surveys, the University of Virginia's James Davison Hunter analyzed students and faculty at sixteen evangelical institutions. "Most (67%)," says Hunter of those he polled, "claimed that the first reason they would give a nonbeliever" for accepting the gospel "would be either the 'sense of meaning and purpose in life' coming from being a Christian or the fact that 'God has made a difference in my life.'" Furthermore, says Hunter, "Virtually half (46%)" of the evangelical seminary students "felt that under most circumstances," to tell people they would go to hell unless they repented was "in poor taste."[23] In other words, the problems Christianity is supposed to solve in the pragmatic gospel are different from the concerns Christians used to have.

It is quite true that some aspects of personal evangelism have been condescending, judgmental, and rude. Obviously, one ought not to walk up to a complete stranger and ask him, "Do you know you're going to hell?" Nevertheless, that is the problem and one cannot presume to have passed along the gospel if "the difference God made in my life," a man-centered, pragmatic focus, has replaced the concern of being reconciled to God.

Marty comments on the absence of the older doctrinal driving force: "People pick and choose truths as if on a cafeteria line, until they get the right diet or mixture."[24] I hear people frequently say, "I'm a 'Calminian'" (a Calvinist-Arminian blend), or, "I like to keep a balance between grace and works." The comfortable place to be is in the middle of two mutually exclusive points of view. Again, the reason is simple: true or not, it works.

We must not compete with the world in offering panaceas. For once one discovers the oasis to be nothing more than a mirage, that person is more certain than before that Christianity is useless. We must resist the pragmatic gospel: Look at these movie stars, successful businessmen, and athletes—Christianity worked for them! Give Jesus a chance! Even prayer, in that scheme, becomes a technique for manipulating God, rather than a personal relationship: "I discovered the reality of that dynamic dimension in prayer that comes through visualizing," declared Robert Schuller. "Don't try to understand it. Just start to enjoy it! It's true. It works. I tried it."[25]

So does Christianity have to offer a better program for self-esteem for it to deserve wide market approval? Maybe a better method of child-rearing or a greater incentive for moral improvement? I'm tired of hearing sermons on "How to Have an Effective Quiet Time" or "How to Get More Out of Your Christian Life." Don't offer me another list of "Four Steps to Victorious Christian Living." I've tried them all and not only do they fail to answer the deeper questions; they don't even work for the superficial ones. "I want to know *Christ* and the power of his resurrection and the fellowship of sharing in his sufferings, becoming like him in his death, and so somehow, to attain to the resurrection from the dead" (Phil. 3:10–11, italics added). That may not answer everybody's thirst for the practical, but it's refreshing in an age of false claims and defective mail-order saviors.

Consumerism ③

We must stop reducing the God of the universe to
something we can sell to people.
—Gregory Lewis, *Is God for Sale?*

In the popular movie *Risky Business*, there is a scene in
which Joel (played by Tom Cruise) and some of his friends
are eating at the corner hamburger stand. Joel, feeling the
pressures of materialism all around him, asks, "Is all everybody wants to do is make money?" His friends, stunned by
what they perceive as a stupid question, say, in chorus,
"Yes." "A *lot* of money," adds one friend. "What about you,
Joel?" There is a pause in which one is left wondering how
Joel will answer, and then he responds, "I want to serve my
fellow man." Immediately aware of how out of step his
answer is, Joel grins, betraying the seriousness of his answer,
and everyone laughs, at ease having gotten the "joke."

Later in the movie, Joel meets a prostitute to whom he is
attracted. He is becoming more in step with things and
realizes the "virtues" he sees in the prostitute: "No guilt, no
doubts, no fear. Just the shameless pursuit of immediate

material gratification—what a capitalist!" By the end of the movie, Joel has built an empire of ill repute, only to have it topple. Joel shows us how he handled the pressure: "My name is Joel Goodson. I deal in human fulfillment. I grossed over eight thousand dollars in one night. Time of your life, huh kid?"

One wonders if we have exploited God the way Joel exploited himself and the women he sold in the competitive market of immediate gratification. Do we, like Joel, "deal in human fulfillment," purveying divine merchandise for the purpose of satisfying the market instead of the Creator? And are we willing to engage at least marginally in false advertising to make a sale? Aristotle said, "Fables are suitable for addresses to popular assemblies; and they have one advantage—they are comparatively easy to invent."

Historian Jackson Lears reports that "to thrive and spread, a consumer culture required more than a national apparatus of marketing and distribution; it also needed a favorable moral climate" *(From Salvation to Self-Realization)*. It seems that evangelicalism not only failed to discourage the exploitation of God and man, but actually advanced it, exchanging the Creator-creature relationship for that of Producer-consumer.

The late-nineteenth-century evangelist Dwight L. Moody was a shoe salesman prior to his conversion—and a good one. He was to take his sales approach to his evangelistic enterprise, insisting that he was still a salesman as an evangelist; he had just switched products.[1] Later, after the turn of the century, Billy Sunday would turn the platform into a stage and boast that he was "the most efficient evangelist and guaranteed results at two dollars per soul."[2]

Before both Moody and Sunday, Charles Finney, the father of "new measures" in evangelism, said, "A revival is not a miracle, or dependent on a miracle in any sense. It is a purely philosophic result of the right use of means."[3] This pragmatic approach, which we studied in chapter 2, created a businesslike approach which took the gospel one step further from the God-centered evangelism of Jonathan

Edwards and George Whitefield. Now the gospel not only had to work; it had to sell. The Industrial Revolution turned the evangelist into a mechanic; the capitalist revolution turned the evangelist into a businessman. Either way, the gospel was no longer "the power of God for . . . salvation" (Rom. 1:16), but "the right use of means" necessary to make the sale.

Finney said that the Christian religion "is the work of man. . . . It consists in obeying God. It is man's duty."[4] It was a short step from this sort of theology to its commercial reduction. Selling a person on Jesus was similar to selling a person on a particular pair of shoes. The attractiveness of the pitch made the sale. Jesus was the product, the sinner was the consumer, and the evangelist was the packaging and marketing agent. In this scheme, humans are buyers instead of debtors.

One has to spend no more than an hour or two at one of the larger evangelical trade conventions to feel the uneasiness of an Alice in a wonderland of trinkets and "Jesus junk." We have made our sovereign Lord about as cheap as the hairbrush that has his name stamped on it. Yet, as Gregory Lewis notes, "God is not a product to be pushed, but a King to be obeyed." Sinners do not buy him as they would a new self-improvement program. Instead, sinners renounce themselves and embrace the Savior. Jesus is not there to fill whatever is lacking in our self-esteem or our self-fulfillment. He is there to slay our self-confidence and to place our confidence in him alone (Jer. 17:5, 7; Phil. 3:3).

Nevertheless, we are told, the gospel has to sell. There is a great deal of competition these days, so we must package and manage this enterprise with maximum strategy. Therefore, evangelism must shape the evangel. The method must determine the message. The numbers game dominates the minds and nerves of most pastors and parachurch executives these days. There are actually seminars, institutes, and year-around schools training Christian leaders in church growth strategies. Some of these people have never taken a class in theology, but they have their neighborhood's demographics and "felt needs" memorized. Superchurches and superprograms come complete with the superpastors, the spiritual Hercules everyone looks up to. Football stars, beauty queens, and movie stars become the evangelical theologians and spokespersons. It is, after all, more interesting to hear simplistic formulas about Jesus improving one's running game than being taught the Scriptures by someone who works part time at the bowling alley.

Books about God's promises (including ones he has yet to make) far outsell books about God himself. The gifts, it seems, are more interesting, than the Giver.

Power Sells

During the "Year of the Bible" (1983), the nation was inundated with the "power for living" campaign. In the book by that title, offered by celebrities via television commercials, one notices the single thread running throughout: Jesus is the best self-improvement program around. Everyone wants success and power; therefore, that is one more "felt need" for which Christianity must provide a satisfying product. Businessmen and women have their power programs, politicians have theirs, and now the church is to offer spiritual power as a supplement. We must not displease people with negative teaching about sin and guilt, nor burden them with theology about grace and justification, election, and the substitutionary atonement. How does a gospel which proclaims "when we were still powerless, Christ died for the ungodly" (Rom. 5:6) sell to an audience that does not want to be told it is powerless? Our power-minded neighbors don't want to be told, "You were dead in your transgressions and sins. . . . God . . . made us alive with Christ even when we were dead in transgressions" (Eph. 2:1, 4, 5). The last thing they want to hear is, "It does not depend on man's desire or effort, but on God's mercy" (Rom. 9:16). But that is exactly the point the gospel is making and must make.

In the movie *Power*, Richard Gere plays an enterprising

media wizard who presents Washington's most powerful candidates to the public. Image is all that matters. Surveys are exhaustively reviewed to determine what popular beliefs and attitudes can be exploited (I will refrain from making a nasty comparison to certain church-growth strategies). "It doesn't matter who's running the show," says Gere, "just the show." After turning even hopeless cases into elected officials, Gere takes on a genuine crusader for the betterment of society. The man's authenticity wears Gere down until he realizes the long-term significance of even short-term failures: "We're irrelevant," he explains. "But you'll stay. Candidates are prepackaged, predigested, like TV dinners; I've made a lot of money believing that." Finally, Gere, puzzled, concludes, "Something human came into this race—some honesty, something that wasn't slick and prepackaged, something that wasn't engineered by these media wizards."

It could be said of no one more appropriately than of Christ, "Something human came into this race, something that wasn't slick and prepackaged, something that wasn't engineered by media wizards." Nevertheless, the religious media wizards continue to do to Jesus Christ what Gere's character had been doing to his candidates—creating salable saviors, exploiting public emotions and fears.

The Gospels reveal a Savior who entered reality and was interested in that reality, not in images. The world was fallen, in a state of rebellion, chaos, despair. His realism took him to the cross. Jesus was hardly one to engineer reality. Because he told the truth, he lost disciples, was threatened, and was crucified. But evangelicals, it seems, have gotten used to the television cameras and press coverage. The last thing we seem to be ready for is unpopularity.

The defect is not in a short-sighted methodology with too much media wizardry, but that our "gospel" itself is consumer-centered rather than God-centered. This is the religious legacy inherited from our Arminian and Enlightenment past: human-centeredness. It is as if God must be justified before the sinner; the sinner has to be satisfied with God and his terms. The ancient gospel was always concerned with how God could be satisfied with us, through the sacrifice of Christ in our place.

We can see how each of the philosophical characteristics of American religion build on each other. First, we declared independence from all sovereigns, including God, and established a religion, as well as a culture, "of the people, for the people, and by the people." The biblical God celebrated by the Reformation was a monarch who elected his citizens and ruled his kingdom. The democratic god celebrated by the American people was a civil servant who was elected by the people to serve their interests. The biblical God was told he could remain in our company only so long as he stayed on the sidelines and served as a public mascot—not as an umpire, nor even as a player, but as a mascot.

Then, pragmatism demanded that God serve not only as mascot, but also as bellhop. God had to work and his own revelation had to meet the approval of utilitarian interests. We began fashioning an American god in earnest and "worshiped and served created things rather than the Creator" (Rom. 1:25). And now, human-centered religion takes another step toward supposed autonomy by demanding that God be a product, too.

Is the gospel, then, a matter of supply and demand? Yes, if it is God who is doing the demanding. God demands that we either conform to his law or be banished forever. And yet, no one can conform to that standard, so God himself provides the supply for this demand. His own Son lives a perfect life of law-keeping, bears God's wrath for our lawlessness, and through his resurrection imputes to the believing wicked that perfect obedience and righteousness.

The Great Commission

Our Lord's command was to "go and make disciples of all nations, baptizing them in the name of the Father and of the Son and of the Holy Spirit, and teaching them to obey everything I have commanded you" (Matt. 28:19–20). This is a God-centered commission. There is nothing here about adapting our presentation to the "felt needs" of our audience. After all, Saint Paul said the gospel was "a stumbling block to Jews and foolishness to Gentiles" (1 Cor. 1:23). "For the wisdom of this world is foolishness in God's sight. . . . So then, no more boasting about men!" (3:19, 21).

Of course, this does not mean that we ought to ignore the realities of contemporary struggles or the context in which the gospel is presented. Nevertheless, what we get from Scripture is that there is a real sense in which the gospel is not supposed to sell! If we succeed in making the gospel appealing to sinners on the basis of satisfying their consumer appetites, we have not succeeded at all. If unbelievers do not find Christianity offensive (that is, for the right reasons), there is something wrong with our presentation. The Great Commission was a command to make disciples, not to establish franchises for consumers.

"Jesus' Church-Shrinkage Program"

My friend and seminary professor, W. Robert Godfrey, coined this phrase in referring to our Lord's evangelistic strategy in John 6. The five thousand who got a free lunch rented every boat on the lake to cross over to find Jesus. And yet, Jesus was troubled with the size of the crowd. This is the first lesson from this passage: We ought to be suspicious of huge crowds. This doesn't mean that we exert ourselves to keep the church small. Obviously, we want as many people to become Christians as possible! Nevertheless, crowds and popularity ought to make us wonder about whether people are following for the right reasons.

So often I hear brothers and sisters say of a television evangelist, "You can't condemn that man's ministry—look how many souls he's reaching!" Of course, that is one of the main reasons I'm so worried! Gregory Lewis notes, "Wanting to stand out, wanting to feel important—and this is a basic desire of human nature—the Church pours on the heat with futile efforts and hasty works. In a state of panic, churches climb to the heap of humanity, raise their hands, and cry: 'But we're winning souls!'"[5] While "four billion served" may justify McDonald's existence, "four billion saved" is not a worthy goal for Christianity if we have to amend the gospel and hence create consumers rather than disciples. But then, only disciples are saved.

In this passage, then, how does Jesus respond to those who began to follow after the feeding of the five thousand? He says, you follow me "not because you saw miraculous signs but because you ate the loaves and had your fill" (John 6:26). In other words, "You are not converts, but consumers. You're like stray cats that follow, not out of any attachment to a new owner, but because they remember who fed them last." Then, Jesus, unwilling to gather a crowd of consumers, begins to preach one of his most unpopular sermons. First, he tells people that their real problem is not physical hunger. Instead of exploiting "felt needs," Jesus challenges them: Is that really your deepest, most immediate problem? Is it not the case that you are only following me because doing so worked for you yesterday?

Second, Jesus tells them that he is the solution to the problem which they have ignored. "I am the living bread that came down from heaven," he announced (v. 51). "Unless you eat the flesh of the Son of Man and drink his blood, you have no life in you" (v. 53). What an exclusive and bigoted message! The Jews were children of Abraham, heir to the promises. Who was this Rabbi who dared to tell Israel she had no life unless she embraced this man from Nazareth? Then Jesus continues: "Stop grumbling among yourselves. . . . No one can come to me unless the Father who sent me draws him, and I will raise him up at the last day" (vv. 43–44). "On hearing" this message, John writes, "many of his disciples said, 'This is a hard teaching. Who can accept it?" (v. 60). But Jesus pushed still further: "Aware that his disciples were grumbling about this, Jesus said to them, 'Does this offend you? What if you see the Son of Man ascend to where he was before! The Spirit gives life;

the flesh counts for nothing. . . . This is why I told you that no one can come to me unless the Father has enabled him'" (vv. 61–63, 65). John records the response: "From this time many of his disciples turned back and no longer followed him. 'You do not want to leave too, do you?' Jesus asked the Twelve. Simon Peter answered him, 'Lord, to whom shall we go? You have the words of eternal life. We believe and know that You are the Holy One of Israel'" (vv. 66–69).

Jesus didn't tailor his message to suit the audience. He challenged their presuppositions, concluding, "If you are too proud for this sort of radical solution, what if I went back to heaven and left you to yourselves?" It's either that, or the humiliating confession, "The Spirit gives life"—God does the saving, "the flesh counts for nothing." By modern standards, that was one of the greatest evangelistic failures in church history. But there were twelve left, eleven of whom became the foundation of the church and died martyrs for a faith worth dying for.

Prior to the feeding of the five thousand, Saint John noted that "a great crowd of people followed him because they saw the miraculous signs" (John 6:2). While miracles attested to Christ's mission and authority, he often characterized the attraction to miracles as a lack of faith rather than its demonstration. Note carefully the following scene: "As the crowds increased, Jesus said, 'This is a wicked generation. It asks for a miraculous sign'" (Luke 11:29). "As the crowds increased," Jesus changed his strategy to proclaiming a gospel which upset what the people had felt and believed their entire lives.

A significant part of selling today's gospel is the appeal to the sensational. It not only has to come with a money-back guarantee that it will work (the five thousand looking for a free lunch); it has to dazzle the audience (the "wicked generation" seeking miracles). The call to die to self is replaced with the invitation to add Jesus to the other products we use for self-fulfillment. Television is particularly vulnerable to abuse in evangelism. It is a persuasive, glamorous medium in its own right. I've been on secular talk shows and there is a tremendous power. I can also understand why Malcolm Muggeridge framed Christ's temptation by Satan as an offer of going on television.

Furthermore, television advertising can often create a false need. While watching a television commercial advertising a remedy for balding, I found myself for a brief moment needing this cure. There was only one problem: I'm not losing any hair yet. Advertising in general can create momentary artificial needs. When emotion-centered folk religion gets its own television shows, the church settles for momentary consumers. Jesus spoke to no more than thirty thousand people during his life, and his disciples can be found today among the most remote tribes. Today's television preachers speak to millions every week, and I have yet to find one person who accepted the gospel through the electronic church. (I have, however, met people who were put off because of it.)

Christian programing can sell viewers an attractively (if falsely) packaged gospel—and it can manipulate viewers at least momentarily into becoming consumers. But the task of making disciples is ignored by the leading televangelists, and one wonders if the medium itself allows for the possibility of assisting in that effort. Disciples need to be formed over an extended period of time by neighbors, not images. New believers need to see the beliefs they are learning as they are practiced by people who are a phone call away.

In a popular 1987 film, *Mosquito Coast*, there is a poignant scene in which we hear the voice of a televangelist invading the silence of a remote South American rain forest. The camera continues toward the missionary church until it finally focuses on the natives inside the church—watching the missionary on a large screen. While I was offended at the false representation of missionaries, that reminded me of the advertisements I saw in evangelical media periodicals marketing a new church-growth strategy which featured a leading televangelist each Sunday. The ad offered a package which included installation of a satellite dish and the benefit of a celebrity pastor indefinitely. In this case, the truth was indeed stranger than fiction.

What was the church-growth strategy of Acts? The proclamation and exposition of Scripture ("they were continually devoting themselves to the apostles' teaching"), commitment to community ("they had everything in common"), the frequent administration of communion ("the breaking of bread"), and church discipline (as amply demonstrated by the Holy Spirit's slaying of Ananias and Sapphira). One pastor of a superchurch, responding to questions in *Christianity Today*, attributed the superchurch to the fact that "people have different tastes. The larger church," he added, "has the people and the resources to provide a variety of ministries and services that care for the total needs of the family, which a smaller church cannot do."[6] What is Saint Luke's explanation of the growth of that early church? "And the *Lord* added to their number daily those who were being saved" (Acts 2:47, italics added).

Trivial Pursuits

It has happened to some of our favorite artists. In the beginning, their painting, sculpture, or music is exquisite. While their fans were few, their love for the craft outweighed commercial pressures. But, to reach and satisfy a broader audience, the artist had to trivialize. Once servants of their art, they have become slaves of the market.

The same is true in politics. We have watched men and women who really had something to say dilute their message with vague slogans. In fact, ambiguity is essential for popularity. And ambiguity trivializes. Not long ago, I tried to get a religion writer for a major newspaper to attend a theological debate. The reporter (a friend of mine) confessed that it wouldn't be worth his while, since, he cynically observed, evangelical leaders find it almost impossible to deal with doctrinal issues which might alienate part of their following. "They're worse than politicians," he said. He is not an evangelical, but I am, and I deeply regret the impression made in the mind of that reporter.

In the struggle to market Christianity, modern sales representatives have accommodated this reduction of Christianity. In consumer religion, Christianity becomes trivialized. Its great mysteries become cheap slogans. Its majestic hymns are traded in for shallow jingles, often sung off the image from an overhead projector, much like an advertising executive uses to sell a client on an ad campaign. And its parishioners, now unashamedly called audiences, have come to expect dazzling testimonies, happy anecdotes, and fail-proof schemes for successful living that will satiate spiritual consumption.

Products must be trivialized if they are going to sell well and widely. Mass marketing almost always reduces the quality of the product. To stand out among other competing wares, Christianity is reduced to relying on quick, catchy, attractive packaging.

A More Fundamental Question

This brings us to the question, *Should* the gospel sell? It is clear that we should not shape the gospel like a wax nose to suit the tastes of fallen men and women. But the Bible poses a more fundamental question: Is the gospel supposed to sell?

Saint Paul said, "The man without the Spirit does not accept the things that come from the Spirit of God, . . . and he cannot understand them" (1 Cor. 2:14). Conversion is the result of the Word and Spirit, not of human manipulation. Therefore, without the Word, there can be only consumers, never disciples. The gospel is characterized in the New Testament as "an offense," but the gospel being preached today is anything but offensive. The cross is generally adopted as a popular symbol. It is worn by pimps and pornographers, serial murderers and rapists, and is illuminated by some unscrupulous preachers. The writhing body hanging in agony, crying, "My God, my God, why have you forsaken me?" doesn't offend people these days—due in part to the fact that what is preached most often these days is not "Christ and him crucified" (1 Cor. 2:2).

"The new cross," wrote A. W. Tozer, "does not slay the sinner; it redirects him. It shows him a jollier and cleaner way to live. To the assertive, the new cross says, 'Come assert yourself for the Lord!'"[7] And, we might add, to the smart shopper, the new cross says, "Have I got a deal for you. If you are not completely satisfied, simply return it for a full refund."

A gospel that suits the tastes of people who are alienated from God and "dead in . . . transgressions and sins" (Eph. 2:1) is not the gospel found in the Bible. The gospel's starting place is not, "God loves you and has a wonderful plan for your life," as though the unbeliever's problem is a lack of education in God's love and a lack of spiritual and moral direction. Rather, the gospel begins with a deeper problem and, hence, a deeper solution. "Whoever believes in him is not condemned, but whoever does not believe stands condemned already because he has not believed in the name of God's one and only Son" (John 3:18).

Conclusion

We are not selling a product to a consumer, but proclaiming a Savior to a sinner. Commercial evangelism may bring attention to us, but the evangelical revival we have been hearing about is just another movement. Wait until the bright lights burn out and the superchurches are turned into warehouses as the next generation grows more cynical than it would otherwise have been. What happens when the churches can no longer keep up with the technological sophistication of the entertainment industry? In short, what happens when the loaves and fishes run out?

Erich Fromm mused, "Modern man, if he dared to be articulate about his concept of heaven, would describe a vision which would look like the biggest department store in the world" *(The Sane Society)*. One wonders if some of us, perhaps all of us, attend church with the same consumer goals nurtured by another temple—the shopping mall. Churches used to be selected by a family on the basis of being the preferred church in the neighborhood, but church-hopping has become a modern hobby.

Bear in mind the Lord's judgment of the church in Laodicea (Rev. 3:17): "You say, 'I am rich; I have acquired wealth and do not need a thing.' But you do not realize that you are wretched, pitiful, poor, blind and naked." In other words, "When it comes to material 'needs,' your prayer list is the length of three football fields, but when it comes to your spiritual needs, you are so self-assured. You are still consumers rather than disciples. You are wretched; I will wash you as white as snow. You are pitiful, but I will have pity on whom I will have pity. And in spite of your pretensions, you are poor; I will grant you the riches of my grace." Finally, "Though you pretend to own your own wardrobe, you really are naked, but I will clothe you in my own righteousness."

Let's make sure we are content with nothing less than to be clothed with Christ and his righteousness. Let's not settle for less than God's best and his glory. Jesus Christ is not a product or technique, but a person. And he is "not sold in any stores." He cannot be bought. Rather it was we "who have been bought with a price"—the price of Christ's life. And his death guarantees God's satisfaction.

In the sixteenth century, a Dominican preacher named John Tetzel went from town to town selling indulgences—pardons for offenses—for a small price. "When the coin in the coffer rings, a soul from purgatory springs," Tetzel's traveling choir sang. Martin Luther's Ninety-Five Theses were prompted by the shamelessness of Rome's consumerism. "This same Tetzel, then," Luther snapped, "carried indulgences about and sold grace for money." Selling grace for money is not a foreign idea to today's merchants of souls. In his hit, made popular during the Pearlygate scandal, Ray Stevens sings of our modern Tetzels, "They sell you salvation while they sing 'Amazing Grace.'"

It is time now that we rescue the cross, that cruel, bloodstained stumbling block, and the priceless quality of a Savior who isn't for sale.

From Salvation to Self-Esteem 4

For Men and Women Who Want to Achieve Their
Maximum Potential
—ad for the Word of Faith World Outreach Center

We used to think that the good news of the gospel was
that sinners could be saved, or salvaged, from the wreckage
of original and personal sin. Today, it seems, there is a new
focus. In the old gospel, the problem was, "How does a holy
God accept sinners?" For the new one, the problem appears
to be, "How do basically good people accept themselves?"
—a shift indeed.

But, this is where society is today. And as society goes,
so goes the church. Malcolm Gladwell, a writer for the
Washington Post, observes, "Even as it has been in reaction
to secular America, fundamentalist culture has shown a
marked ability to adapt to social trends." Nathan Hatch, a
historian at Notre Dame, adds, "They spoke the language
of peace of mind in the 1950s, developed a theology of
'body life' and community in the wake of the 1960s, and

73

are currently infatuated with a gospel of self-esteem that
correlates precisely with the contemporary passion for self-
fulfillment."[1]

In this chapter, I want to outline some of the ways in
which we evangelicals have given in to one of Lucifer's
most powerful illusions: self-fulfillment. This illusion appears
in three shapes, hedonism, narcissism, and materialism.

Hedonism

A popular bumper sticker sports this proverb: "He who
dies with the most toys wins." A similar one counsels,
"When the going gets tough, the tough go shopping."
Advertisements lure us into buying products "because I
believe in me"; they insist I can "have it my way," that I
"deserve a break today," and that the only person I have to
please is myself. Our affluent society has an obvious attraction for solving some of its problems by satiating the desire
to possess things. Tammy Faye Bakker confessed on ABC's
"Nightline" that her compulsive shopping was "for my
nerves. It sure beats a psychiatrist." One might say we are
consumed by consumption.

Many of our debates concerning America's economic crisis make a good deal of the fact that America is consuming
more than it is producing, owing more than it is earning: "I
owe, I owe, so off to work I go." Puritan ethics, even when
secularized, once heavily influenced American enterprise
and trade and emphasized producer traits rather than consumer traits: thrift, hard work, industry, savings, invest-
ment, self-discipline, modesty, and charity. These have
given way to a more secularized, self-centered outlook in
the context of social Darwinism's survival of the fittest.

For the Puritans, and for Protestants generally, the pursuit
of pleasure as an end in itself was the pursuit of godlessness.
While they were not grim killjoys (as they are often carica-
tured), they had a sober suspicion about self-indulgence.
According to the English sociologist Colin Campbell,
"Puritanism, if not Protestantism in general, must surely

rank as one of the most powerful anti-hedonistic forces which the world has known."[2] Campbell adds:

> We can see from this that Puritanism did not attempt to banish all pleasure from life; "rational recreation" was permitted. . . . In this context, they did not prohibit alcohol, as their nineteenth-century successors, the evangelicals, were to strive so hard to do. Nor, for example, did they uphold the Catholic ideal of celibacy; continence was a virtue, but abstinence was in conflict with God's commands. Hence their clergy married young and often, and women had a right to expect more from their husbands than duty. In fact, as Carroll observes, the Puritans did a good deal to promote a "new fusion of sensual and spiritual love in marriage."[3]

Campbell points to the English Civil War, contrasting the luxury- and consumption-oriented Royalists who supported Charles's absolute monarchy and the moderation- and production-oriented Puritans who ended up winning the day, at least for a while. "But," he adds, "it was the new intellectual climate created by the Arminian revolt which made [the shift from excess to moderation] possible."[4] Of course, it would be painting with a broom to suggest that Arminianism is the source of hedonism in American life, or that it is the source of all our woes. Nevertheless, any theology which compromises the centrality of God, his sovereignty and grace, runs the risk of replacing the center with man. And that has a multitude of effects in every practical sphere. When one has declared that man's good rather than God's glory is the goal of salvation (which English and American Arminianism clearly said), it is not a large step from that to incipient hedonism.

If the thesis that Arminianism helped nurture hedonism sounds a bit overstated, we have only to remind ourselves that historians unanimously agree that the driving force behind the Protestant (often called "Puritan") work ethic is Calvinism. This is not to say that one should always expect an Arminian to be a hedonist and a Calvinist to be a hard-working sort. In many lives, the roles are reversed.

Nevertheless, there is a direct and well-documented influence which Reformed theology has exercised in shaping the values of a people who could withstand the rigors of a wilderness in the pursuit of "ye glory of God and ye advancement of ye Christian faythe."

As Christians began to think less theologically and more sentimentally, they were less motivated by the aim "to glorify God and enjoy him forever" than by the pursuit of happiness. Today, we have a gospel of health, wealth, and happiness. We no longer exist for God's happiness and glory (esteem), but he for ours. This attitude is reflected even in the name of a church: The Happy Church.

Jimmy Carter wrote, "American people are living lives that are wasteful, self-indulgent, purposeless, and meaningless. There is a crisis of spirit." But those are the "unsaved," the worldly and godless secular humanists who are narcissistic, hedonistic and materialistic, aren't they? Not so. Carl F. H. Henry, America's foremost evangelical leader, states, "American evangelicalism is being spiritually thwarted by its affluence. No group of Christians has . . . more to learn about sacrifice. Our lifestyles are clearly non-Christian . . . marked by greed, extravagance, self-gratification, and lack of compassion for the needy."[5]

Pollsters George Barna and William P. McKay lament: "Survey data supply ample evidence of the bankruptcy of the commonly held world views of Christians. It is undeniable that as a body, American Christians have fallen prey to materialism, hedonism, . . . and even to a jaded form of Christianity that rejects much of the commitment required of faithful servants."[6] According to these pollsters, "A recent national survey discovered that no fewer than seven out of ten Christians are prone to hedonistic attitudes about life. A similar proportion of born-again people," they say, "deny the possibility that pain or suffering could be a means of becoming a better, more mature individual." Then, "as a final example, three out of ten Christians agree that 'nothing in life is more important than having fun and being happy.'"[7]

Thus, the criterion for religion is that it must make me happy. It must be fun and exciting. Of course, we humans have held hedonistic attitudes about life ever since the fall, so we have to be careful about making sweeping judgments concerning our own age; nevertheless, it hardly seems inappropriate to recognize an acute problem in contemporary Christianity.

In his best-seller, *Reagan's America,* political writer Garry Wills distinguished the Reagan era from the Carter presidency:

> The contrast with Carter is not in *degree* of belief but in *what* they believe. There are different theologies at work. Carter's in some ways is more modern. . . . But he [Carter] is comparatively old-fashioned in his theology; too old-fashioned, in fact, in the eyes of evangelicals themselves, who deserted him for Reagan in 1980.
>
> Carter's religion is what William James called that of the "sick soul"—a religion of man's fall, of the need for repentance, of humility. In its Calvinistic form, this "classical" religion was important in the early history of America. But America has increasingly preferred the religion James called "healthy-mindedness," which replaces sin with sadness as the real enemy of human nature. The modern evangelicals, beaming and healthy successes in the communications industry, are exemplars of that religion.[8]

Wills goes on to point out that Americans disdain humility . . . religiously. "More profoundly," he writes, "the imperative to 'feel good about oneself' has become a national and personal priority" which has enlisted evangelical no less than nonevangelical yuppies. "It has become a patriotic, even religious, duty."[9]

"We the people" has led in our own generation to "I the person." Often our communities are collections of individuals who are brought together only in matters of mutual self-interest. Christopher Lasch characterizes this attitude in *The Culture of Narcissism:* "Self-absorption, according to Marin, insulates affluent Americans against the horrors around them—poverty, racism, injustice—and 'eases their troubled conscience.' Schur attacks the 'awareness craze' on the grounds that it addresses problems peculiar to the well-to-do. . . . But the self-preoccupation on which the awareness movement capitalizes arises not from complacency but from desperation."[10]

It is a sad day for the church when secular commentators point out society's self-absorption as a short-sighted attempt to "ease their troubled conscience," while many leading evangelicals appear to be missing that point. Evangelicals should be the first to recognize the symptoms and to diagnose self-absorption, but they are too much a part of the illness. Robert Schuller laments, "I don't think anything has been done in the name of Christ and under the banner of Christianity that has proven more destructive to human personality, and hence counterproductive to the evangelistic enterprise, than the unchristian, uncouth strategy of attempting to make people aware of their lost and sinful condition."[11] Never mind that Jesus came "to call . . . sinners to repentance" (Luke 5:32) or that he "came to seek and to save what was lost" (Luke 19:10).

As those who must submit our affections to the probing gaze of Scripture, we have an obligation to become people of self-control rather than self-indulgence. The familiar first question of the Westminster Shorter Catechism, "What is the chief end of man?" must be asked again today. And we can only hope for the correct response: "To glorify God and enjoy him forever."

Narcissism

The term *narcissism* is derived from the ancient story of Narcissus, a young Greek athlete who used to go to a pond to admire his reflection. Today, we have mirrors.

It is remarkable how closely America (and the West in general) resembles the ancient Greek and Roman civilizations in their decline. Hedonism (the pleasure cult of Epicureanism) was softening the people into effete consumers who spent more than they produced and who sold the future good of the civilization for immediate comfort and self-gratification. Their pools, baths, and spas fed their craving to be pampered. In fact, some years ago I visited Pompeii, the city preserved by the ash from a volcanic eruption. From the richly ornamented frescoes covering the walls to the spacious spas, Pompeii is a testimony to self-indulgence.

And just as today's crowds huddle in the theater to see heads blown off in increasingly realistic ways, so the Greeks and Romans had their bloody arenas in which cruel spectacles (including, on occasion, the feeding of Christians to lions) entertained the crowds. Alcoholism, homosexuality, and the ethics of self-interest ruled social relations.

Narcissism first surged in the United States with Enlightenment deism. Of course, self-absorption does not come and go with the proper theological prescription. Regardless of how we think, whether we are God-centered in our theology or human-centered, we are nonetheless sinners. And narcissism is the root sin of all others. It *is* the human condition. Yet, in terms of a marked increase in public approval and support for narcissism, the Enlightenment championed, "I am the master of my fate, the captain of my soul." Transcendentalism, though antirationalistic, pursued another, more concentrated phase of narcissism by turning people inward. While the Enlightenment called people to look to themselves, Transcendentalism invited them to look within themselves. To the Enlightenment, god was one's rational mind as it observed nature; to Transcendentalism and Romanticism, god was one's subjective feelings as they experienced nature. Thus, the rugged individual became further isolated from the community, eventually withdrawing into self-contemplation that has found its climax in our own society with its emphasis on therapeutic well-being.

When it comes to narcissism, perhaps no generation has been more intoxicated with it than our own. Popular magazines such as *Harper's* published "The New Narcissism" (by

Peter Marin); a *New Yorker* article by Tom Wolfe pro-
nounced the seventies the "Me Decade." Lasch wrote a
best-seller describing *The Culture of Narcissism* as "the culture
of competitive individualism, which in its decadence has
carried the logic of individualism to the extreme of a war of
all against all, the pursuit of happiness to the dead end of a
narcissistic preoccupation with the self."[12] Ironically, the
most insightful critiques of this disturbing vice have come
from secular rather than evangelical publishing houses.

In a television commercial typical of many, an actress
concedes, "Sure it costs more, but I'm worth it." America's
famous opinion researcher, Louis Harris, notes, "It is not
overstating to report that a solid majority of the American
people are close to being obsessed with their personal
appearance."[13] So what do we do? Why, we write Christian
personal appearance books, of course! These volumes provide noncontextual endorsements from Scripture to show
us how we need to believe in ourselves, love ourselves, rely
on ourselves to a greater degree. From the pagans, it's self-
centeredness, but from our own brethren it's simply "being
everything God meant us to be." After all, we're "King's
kids"! In his unlikely role as God (in *Oh God!*), George Burns
says, "If you find it hard to believe in me, it might help you
to know that I believe in you."

Lasch argues, "Having no hope of improving their lives in
any of the ways that matter, people have convinced themselves that what matters is psychic self-improvement: getting
in touch with their feelings."[14] In this context, God becomes
a therapist and the Bible becomes a devotional guide which
is designed to help people get in touch with their feelings.
The authors of *Habits of the Heart* refer to the sentiment of
one person who epitomizes this outlook: "For her now, God
is 'sort of a name that's been assigned to that particular kind
of function for me, to make the most of my life.'"[15]

Schuller does not even blush when he charges that "classical Reformed theology has erred in its insistence that
theology be God-centered, not man-centered. It was appropriate for Luther and Calvin to think theocentrically," but

now "the scales must tip the other way."[16] For this "new Reformation" of self-esteem, sin is anything "that strips one of God's children of his right to Divine dignity." "Sin," Schuller says, "is any act or thought that robs myself or another human being of his or her self-esteem."[17] Before, of course, sin was robbing God of his due: "Against you, you only, have I sinned," confessed the psalmist (Ps. 51:4). Further, salvation is not reconciliation with a God who has been offended by our rebellion, but "self-esteem rising all around me and within me. . . . I'll really feel good about myself."[18] In his worthy zeal to make the Christian hope practical and relevant, Schuller has sadly "exchanged the truth of God for a lie, and worshiped and served created things rather than the Creator—who is forever praised" (Rom. 1:25). What is Schuller's heaven? It is the quenching of "the person's hunger for glory."[19] And yet, God declares, "I am the LORD; that is my name! I will not give my glory to another or my praise to idols" (Isa. 42:8).

Is it true that "the Christian faith and life is a gospel designed to glorify human beings"?[20] How can a story of rebels whose initial declaration of independence in the garden was an attempt at self-glorification lead us to think this is the gospel? Must Satan be no less obvious than this? Are we really willing to reinterpret the evangel to the point where "God's ultimate objective is to turn you and me into self-confident persons"?[21] Not if Saint Paul correctly reflected the tenor of Scripture when he said, "We . . . put no confidence in the flesh" (Phil. 3:3). And yet, according to Schuller, the purpose of the cross was "to sanctify the ego trip."

Evangelist Lester Sumrall adds, "The human will is sovereign. God will not violate it. . . . You are the one in charge. You are the one who holds the wheel and you do the driving."[22] Paganism, whether polytheistic, pantheistic, panentheistic, or deistic, has never wanted anything more than this. Not to be outdone, the new owner of PTL's Heritage USA, evangelist Morris Cerillo, leads believers in this model prayer: "From this day, the world will not walk on me. The unbeliever will not despise me. I will not be stepped on. I have been made the above and not the beneath because I have hearkened to God and covenanted to walk in obedience."[23] And Kenneth Copeland pushes this heresy to the absurd: "You don't have a god living in you; you *are* one!"[24] No wonder Schuller advises his readers to use as a mantra the words, "I am," "I am."[25] After all, says Copeland, "When I read in the Bible where God tells Moses, 'I AM,' I say, 'Yah, I am, too!'"[26] Aside from the most bizarre cases (Shirley McLaine comes to mind), even our narcissistic, self-obsessed society has not taken self-worship as far as many who are still regarded as representative evangelical spokespersons.

When we tipped the scales from celebrating God's glory and grace to human happiness and capacity for good, hedonism was an inevitable consequence. When evangelicalism left the *soli* (only) out of *Deo gloria* (to God be glory), so essential to the Reformation and Puritan faith, and became a product to be used by consumers in "the pursuit of happiness," it not only failed to restrain the "Me Generation"; it helped foster it.

This is why the theological shift from Reformation realism (God-centeredness) to Arminian optimism is so decisive. Martin Luther pointed out the wide practical implications of one's doctrinal focus: "If I do not know whether God does everything in the matter of salvation, I shall ultimately not know how to pray, to worship, to work, or to do anything. For I shall never know how much to attribute to God and to myself."[27]

Even in circles where obvious narcissism is eschewed, there are still narcissistic tendencies. One example is the emphasis on one's personal relationship with Jesus. Harvard Divinity School's dean, Krister Stendahl, notes that American Christians, in contrast to Christians historically, are obsessed with a "salvation-talk" that is self-centered: "What are you doing for *me*, God; who cares what happens to the larger community?"[28] Martin E. Marty summarizes this view: "being rescued is more important than building the created world or serving others."[29] This religious preoccupation with self rejects the God-centered aim of salvation. John Calvin corrected Cardinal Sadoleto on this score: "It is not very sound theology to confine a man's thoughts so much to himself, and not to set before him, as the prime motive of his existence zeal to illustrate the glory of God. For we are born first of all for God, and not for ourselves . . . " He went on: "It certainly is the part of a Christian man to ascend higher than merely to seek and secure the salvation of his own soul. I am persuaded, therefore, that there is no man imbued with true piety who will not consider as insipid that long and labored exhortation to zeal for heavenly life, a zeal which keeps a man entirely devoted to himself, and does not, even by one expression, arouse him to sanctify the name of God."[30]

Further, as the surveys in *The Habits of the Heart* indicate, most Americans "are troubled by the ideal of self-denial the term 'sacrifice' implied."[31] This, perhaps, is why we are more given to sermons on counting the benefits than on counting the cost. Dallas Seminary professor Thomas Constable writes, "Everyone who believes the gospel believes that Jesus is the Savior (1 Cor. 12:3). But not everyone who believes the gospel realizes that the Savior has the right to be Sovereign over his life."[32] Biblical Christianity has never known a gospel that offered the priesthood of Christ without his additional roles as prophet and king. Once more, the "have it your way" culture has shaped much of modern evangelical faith.

Bellah and his co-authors, commenting on the habits of evangelicals within the context of the larger society, recognize that "there is even a tendency visible in many evangelical circles to thin the biblical language of sin and redemption to an idea of Jesus as the friend who helps us find happiness and self-fulfillment." Ironically, the commentary concludes, "The emphasis on love, so evident within the [evangelical] community, is not shared with the world, except through missionary outreach."[33] Instead of confronting the "Me Generation" with tough talk its adherents would come to respect, we have tailored our message to a perfect fit. And when the quest for self-fulfillment wanes, the baby boomers will find it difficult to distinguish evangelicalism from the self-centered fads they eventually rejected.

An interesting sociological study some years ago scanned the popular inspirational literature from 1875 to 1955. "The [evangelical] literature," the sociologists conclude, "presents a man-centered rather than a God-centered religion. It is preoccupied with power, success, life-mastery, and peace of mind and soul and not with salvation in the older sense of the term."[34] As religion is justified on the basis that it works for us, and must, therefore, be packaged in a way which attracts us, the reorientation of the entire Christian religion in this country is complete. God becomes the tool, the technique for self-centered goals. The study notes that the inspirational literature of the first half of this century emphasizes man's goodness and downplays divine glory, majesty, and power. Subjective religious experience replaces doctrine and ritual, they add. In this study by secular sociologists, the conclusion is obvious: "One can hardly doubt that it is distinctively 'American' and reflects American values, both religious and non-religious."[35]

Richard Niebuhr, a Harvard theologian, observed the bankruptcy of liberal optimism when he wrote that "it tends to define religion in terms of adjustment to divine reality for the sake of gaining power rather than in terms of revelation which subjects the recipient to the criticism of that which is revealed." Thus, "man remains the center of religion and God is his aid rather than his judge and redeemer."[36] But one of the most interesting points of this sociological study is that John Stuart Mill himself, the architect of pragmatism, came to realize that the drive to find a god who works for me, making my own happiness the goal, is the worst way to find happiness: "But I now thought that this end was only to be attained by not making it the direct end. For those only are happy . . . who have their minds fixed on some object other than their own happiness."[37]

Elton Trueblood comments, "Heroes . . . who have cared about justice and truth have not even raised the happiness question at all." Though many of them were "gloriously happy, it is not happiness at which they have aimed. This observation is part of what has long been known as the hedonistic paradox, to the effect that happiness is lost if it is the direct aim of a person's life, whereas it often comes abundantly, provided it is neglected."[38]

Materialism

When George Gallup, Jr., surveyed American religion, he found that the materialistic outlook of our society did not differ significantly between Christians and non-Christians. In perhaps the most materially prosperous nation on earth, "more than half of the Christian public" surveyed by Barna and McKay "believes that they 'never have enough money to buy what they need.'" Furthermore, "one out of four believers claim that 'the more things you have, the more successful you've been.'" Tragically, the survey adds that "the proportion of Christians who affirm these values is equivalent to the proportion of non-Christians who hold similar views."[39]

No longer a religion for the poor, the meek, the downcast and downtrodden, the oppressed and broken, Christianity today is for the rich, the proud, the achievers, the powerful, and the successful . . . or for people who want to be. The "victorious Christian life," though not congruent with the realism of Scripture, is a success-oriented triumphalism that surely works in our "what's-in-it-for-me" society.

The "prosperity gospel," as it has come to be called, even by the preachers who promote it, has captured a wide audience, at least in America, where we can afford a god like this. Nevertheless, no religious movement in the Third World has an influence greater than that of the prosperity evangelists. Robert Schuller, Robert Tilton, Oral Roberts (and his son Richard), Kenneth and Gloria Copeland, Kenneth Hagin, Fred Price, Earl Paulk, Paul and Jan Crouch, Pat Robertson, Morris Cerillo, and many others who occupy the religious airwaves promote this materialistic gospel.

The core of this gold-plated gospel is the slogan "name it, claim it." The Americanization of evangelical faith is taken to the tenth power. Man-centeredness, civil religion, pragmatism, consumerism, narcissism, hedonism, and materialism all blend into one crass, diabolical religion of magic. "If you have twenty thousand folks [angels] working to prosper you," reasons Gloria Copeland, "how long do you think it would take them to make you wealthy?"[40] Hagin goes so far as to say that our Lord's statement, "If you ask me anything . . . " (John 14:14) really means, "If you demand anything. . . ."[41]

The prosperity gospel is appropriate for the "Me Generation." Says evangelist Gloria Copeland, "The Christians should be the wealthiest people on earth!"[42] Husband Kenneth concurs: "Jesus was not poor in His ministry. He had a treasurer! The biggest complaint from people," says the televangelist, "is that all the preachers are wanting money. Do you know the best way to stop that complaint? Give it to them! Don't get into strife with them."[43] It is, after all, an arrangement God has worked out: when one gives, he is activating the law of reciprocity. God is obligated by this law to multiply the believer's prosperity (see Robertson, *The Secret Kingdom*). "You can have what you say," declares Copeland.[44] Like Aladdin, we merely rub the lamp three times and out comes a genie to do our bidding. It would be difficult to caricature the Americanization of evangelicalism; the reality is more grotesque than any caricature.

Do the Scriptures not tell us that "the Lord giveth and the Lord taketh away"? This is the witness of the prophets, apostles, martyrs, and doctors of the church—especially Jesus Christ himself, who was such a negative thinker that he said, "It is easier for a camel to go through the eye of a needle than for a rich man to enter the kingdom of God" (Matt. 19:24).

Conclusion

While the prosperity gospel has certainly not captured the entire evangelical community, it has made inroads. Or perhaps it is the case that the secular materialism of the culture has brought varying degrees of accommodation within evangelicalism, of which the prosperity gospel is an extreme.

Even within mainstream evangelical circles, the prayers for things often outweigh the petition, "Thy kingdom come, Thy will be done." And we've gone quite beyond asking for our daily bread. Further, there is little place, even in the mainstream movement, for suffering and pain. Barna and McKay inform us that, according to an American Resource Bureau survey, "No fewer than seven out of ten Christians are prone to hedonistic attitudes about life. . . . A similar proportion of born-again people deny the possibility that pain or suffering could be a means of becoming a better, more mature individual. . . . As a final example, three out of ten Christians agree that 'nothing in life is more important than having fun and being happy.'"[45] This, of course, is far from Saint Paul's remark that "we rejoice in our sufferings, because we know that suffering produces perseverance; perseverance, character; and character, hope" (Rom. 5:3).

The older theology tended to produce strong character. Harvard's Perry Miller is among the historians who have recognized the relationship between creed and character in early New England. Suffering was part of God's plan; even poverty and ruin could be interpreted as God's love (Job is an example). Suffering and pain did not come as an inexplicable surprise to Calvinists in New England, but were considered part of a rational plan and purpose in which God shapes and molds our character. Contemporary evangelicals, however, don't seem to be as clear on whether God or Satan has ultimate authority in this matter. And, in many cases, explanations for suffering, pain, tragedy, or even the death of a loved one are sought in identifying the moral lapses which must have brought them on. Either way—by attributing suffering to the devil or by attributing it to God's punishment rather than his goodness—we have lost an anchor which our forebears enjoyed and relied upon during wretched trans-Atlantic voyages and devastating winters.

But by the end of the twentieth century, we have become

God's demanding little brats. In church, we must be entertained. Our emotions must be charged. We escaped the
clutches of drugs in order to take the "Jesus trip," so we must
be guaranteed comparable experiences. We must have the
best the world has to offer (after all, we're the "King's kids"),
but we cannot associate with the world. We must be offered
amusing programs—we gave up a lot to become Christians
and what little teaching we do get must cater to our pragmatic, self-centered interests. The preaching must be filled
with clever anecdotes and colorful illustrations, with nothing
more than passing references to doctrine: "I want to know
what this means for me and my daily experience!"

We have forgotten that God is a monarch. He is the King
by whom and for whom all things were made, and by
whose sovereign power they are sustained. We exist for his
pleasure, not he for ours; we are on this earth to entertain
him, to please him, to adore him, to bring him satisfaction,
excitement, and joy. Any gospel which seeks to answer the
question, "What's in it for me?" has it all backwards. The
question is, "What's in it for God?" God did not save us for
our pleasure, but for his. He saved us "not because of anything we have done but because of his own purpose and
grace" (2 Tim. 1:9). While, happily, our salvation works out
in our best interest, its goal is the glory of God and the celebration of his mercy.

Marty cautions evangelicals against castigating the world
for its materialistic preoccupation. "Modern American religion," he says, "has also been very materialistic. Prophets of
positive thinking show how Jesus was in the world to help
people become rich. . . . Mind cures, religion exploited to
produce physical health, cults that catered to individual
egos, churches devoted to the pursuit of success—all these
came to the front" during the nineteenth and twentieth
centuries. "Even conservative evangelical Christians,"
Marty notes, "found it difficult to separate themselves from
what Wall Street or the Pentagon wanted for America." But
he concludes with tragic honesty, "When religion appears,
it is usually to justify the status quo. Few ministers would

last more than a few weeks if they called into question the terms of American self-seeking."[46]

In 2 Timothy 3:1–5, Saint Paul gave a warning that is no less appropriate for our own civilization than it was for Timothy's ministry under Nero: "But mark this: There will be terrible times in the last days. People will be lovers of themselves [narcissists], lovers of money [materialists], boastful, proud, abusive, disobedient to their parents, ungrateful, unholy, without love, unforgiving, slanderous, without self-control, brutal, not lovers of the good, treacherous, rash, conceited, lovers of pleasure rather than lovers of God [hedonists]—having a form of godliness but denying its power. Have nothing to do with them."

Godliness is the fruit of the Spirit. While it can be said that the new Christianity in America "has a form of godliness," in its self-aggrandizing moralism, it "denies its power." It is possible to be moral—indeed, pagan morality is universal. While many Christians today resist the secularization of American society in terms of pornography, school prayer, and other concerns of pagan morality, genuine godliness is far from characteristic of the evangelical community.

The answer, again, is a return to a God-centered theological orientation. Pagan morality can be formed by rules, legislation, resolution, and calls to change our ways, but godly character can be formed only as we are "being transformed by the renewing of [our] minds," as we learn to listen to God's Word and, instead of transforming, are transformed by God's radical revelation.

Feeling's Believing 5

You ask me how I know He lives? He lives within
my heart.
—Alfred Ackley, "He Lives"

If ever a line described modern America in terms of a
personal criterion for judgment, it would be, "Feelings,
nothing more than feelings." Religion today is subjective,
privatized, and personal. This is in keeping with a man-centered, pragmatic, consumerist, narcissistic orientation. Even
in evangelical circles, faith in Christ is often justified, if not
because it works, at least on the basis of subjective religious
experience: "You ask me how I know He lives? He lives
within my heart."

Some of my friends are Mormons and it is sometimes
impossible to reason with them about their faith. It does
not matter to them whether historical and archaeological
evidence clearly contradicts their claims. A "burning in my
bosom" is enough to confirm the truth. And yet, I get the
same sort of reasoning (or lack thereof) from many evangelical brothers and sisters!

When the Enlightenment attacked Christianity's long-

91

held convictions, theology tended to retreat instead of standing up to the rationalist challenge. (The Princeton theologians, most notably B. B. Warfield, represent exceptions.) Immanuel Kant told the world that there are two realms: the noumenal (spiritual and invisible) and the phenomenal (physical and observable), and that although certain of Christianity's truth claims cannot be argued through the use of reason or observable evidence, they are nevertheless true. This fideism (faith in faith) was used by Enlightenment rationalists to relegate Christianity to the world of ideas and by Christian pietists to make their faith more an inward experience than an objective, rational religion.

Many of the architects of what we call theological modernism or liberalism, including Kant himself, had a pietistic background. They were tired of barren doctrinal formulas which had no connection to their personal experience. The warm, exciting truths recovered in the Reformation had become rationalized until they were little more than intellectual exercises and dry propositions. The pietists had a legitimate reaction; nevertheless, Christians became increasingly defined in terms of what they experienced and did or did not do instead of what they believed or denied.

It is important to remember that the fathers of modern liberalism were not anti-Christian or intentionally bent on undermining the faith. Rather, they were, like Friedrich Schleiermacher, the father of modern liberalism, merely defending Christianity before its "cultured despisers." They were trying to show that it was all right to be a Christian, even though it may not be rational. That, after all, said the later pietists, is not the realm with which religion is concerned anyway.

Those we charge with the modernist apostasy simply said, "It doesn't matter if Jesus didn't literally rise from the dead in history. His resurrection occurred in my heart, and that's all that matters." That justification is easy to make when you have been reared to think of religion as being a matter of the heart rather than of the heart and head.

The problem is that evangelicals have a growing allegiance to the modernist solution. I have often said that today's pietists are tomorrow's liberals. That seems an odd comment, since we usually associate with pietism a deep devotion to the Lord and to his Word. But if the Christian faith is not understood in terms of rational doctrinal propositions which can then be experienced and lived, it is impossible to "be prepared to give an answer to anyone who asks you to give the reason for the hope you have" (1 Pet. 3:15). As heirs of peitism, modern liberals rejected the historical and rational basis of faith while retaining the sentiment.

The word Saint Peter uses here for "answer" is *apologia*, which was a term lawyers used to refer to their defense. We must be able to present our case before our contemporaries as a lawyer might present a case before a jury. Can you imagine Perry Mason pacing before the jury, urging them to accept his case on the basis of intuition? And yet, many people rest their eternal souls on an intuitive feeling, without ever hearing or seeking a rational line of argumentation in favor of their convictions. It is easy, with such a weak intellectual foundation, for this sort of faith to give in to the pressures of rationalism. (For example, a person might say that Jesus was a feeling or a source of experience, not a person rooted in documented history. Rudolf Bultmann, in the tradition of German liberalism, distinguished between real history and spiritual [i.e., mythological] history.)

After surveying students at evangelical colleges and seminaries, James Davison Hunter concluded, "There is a shift from a concern with 'what the Bible states' to 'what God is telling us,'" from an objective study of Scripture to a subjective experience. Furthermore, "As respondents themselves put it, even if the Bible stories do contradict themselves or defy historical fact, the integrity of Scripture is 'not really undermined.'"[1] This was precisely the point made by the modernists. In other words, they are saying that the Bible is not concerned with what Kant called the phenomenal world (i.e., what can be observed or explained through reason or the senses). So if it errs on history or science, that does not undermine its integrity.

But, of course, that begs the question: Does such error really not undermine the Bible's integrity? If the Bible is incorrect on a point of historical or scientific fact, can we trust it on any other assertion? The defenders of orthodoxy, such as Warfield and J. Gresham Machen, insisted that an error on any fact would make the Bible unreliable for any answers. For them, the distinction modernists made (and which modern evangelicals seem to have accepted) between rational facts and spiritual facts was artificial and contrived. Either the Bible is accurate in all it addresses or it is to be discarded *en toto*. Trusting a book that deceives me about history and science to tell me the truth about God and salvation looks too much like suicide—intellectual, as well as spiritual.

Is it enough that "something happened and now I know He touched me and made me whole"? Is the experience of Jesus, which is claimed by cultists from every corner of the world, enough to justify its claims? Is the experience of Jesus in my heart (an issue the Bible does not even address) the whole defense we bring to a modern world that wants to know why we insist "He Lives"? Our shift from a rational, objective, extroverted faith to an antirational, subjective, introverted spirituality is not a sign of great faith in the face of rationalism, but of default to modern existentialism.

Before we can understand how we have been affected by these trends, we need to know something of the historical process which produced them. Let's take a brief look, then, at the roots of modern subjectivism.

The Enlightenment

The Enlightenment taught us that each person could find truth by looking at the natural world. If God did in fact exist, he was far removed from "the course of human events." While Christianity had always been a thoroughgoing supernaturalism, the emphasis during the Age of Reason was often placed on empirical observation, apart from divine revelation. As nature was their church, so reason was their bible.

Many architects of the Enlightenment were reacting against a dogmatism which fettered reason to the dictates of the church. Though many churchmen picked up Enlightenment ideas in Protestant lands, it was primarily atheists and infidels in Roman Catholic France who created the chief articles of Enlightenment faith. The Reformation was proof that the infallibility of the church could be resisted; the rationalists wanted to go a step further and overthrow revelation as well.

Christians had long held a tremendous interest in the natural world. In fact, it was the orthodox (e.g., Isaac Newton and Blaise Pascal) who were moved by contemplation of a rational, creative God to find the unity, order, and meaning of his creation. The Bible and science (revelation and reason) were not yet engaged in the rivalry we have inherited, but were viewed as two sides of the same coin. The world tells us about God, and common grace makes it possible for anyone, Christian or non-Christian, to decipher truth from error on many issues. The orthodox defended God's existence, not by explaining away, but by using the evidence from nature: the argument from design, from cause, and so on.

Of course, what one does with that evidence depends on God's grace, since unbelievers "suppress the truth by their wickedness" (Rom. 1:18), even though "what may be known about God is plain to them" in creation (v. 19).

Enlightenment thinkers, however, decided that revelation would have to defer to reason. Reason and revelation would always have conflicting answers and in such cases reason should win the day. At this time, the orthodox were divided between the often dead state churches and the pietists; the latter decided that, in a war between reason and revelation, they would choose revelation. Herein was the rationalist victory. We were duped into believing that such a war exists. When we believed that, we lost more than a battle. We surrendered.

Intuitive Individualism

Self-confident subjectivism was further nurtured in America by rugged individualism. As Appalachian religion began to evidence this individualistic folk religion, the sense of confessional community, connection with the past, and rational religious convictions began to disintegrate.

Writing during the early nineteenth century, the French commentator Alexis de Tocqueville observed, "Less attention, I suppose, is paid to philosophy in the United States than in any other country of the civilized world. The Americans have no school of philosophy peculiar to themselves, and they pay very little attention to the rival European schools. Indeed they hardly know their names." And yet, "It is noticeable that the people of the United States almost all have a uniform method . . . of intellectual inquiries. To escape from imposed systems," he says, is the goal. "To seek by themselves and in themselves for the only reason for things, looking to results without getting entangled in the means toward them." Tocqueville adds, "So each man is narrowly shut up in himself, and from that basis makes the pretension to judge the world. . . . So the Americans have needed no books to teach them philosophic method, having found it in themselves."[2]

While the Enlightenment contributed to a shift from a God-centered, supernatural outlook to a man-centered, naturalistic outlook, post-Puritan Americans never accepted either revelation or reason as the arbiter of truth; instead they placed intuition in the seat of judgment. Intuition is "immediate and instinctive perception of truth; direct understanding without reasoning."[3] Each American had his own brand of philosophy which he never really worked out. A simple farmer could organize his own sect without conforming to or even referring to a system of beliefs or rituals. Cults and sects proliferated during the nineteenth century. It was noted that "by 1833, a wag in Illinois reported that a zealous revivalist was 'bellowing and blowing through the Bible, shedding no more light upon the passages quoted than the roar of artillery does upon our Declaration of Independence.'"[4]

This intuitive individualism is prominent in the shift from the Great Awakening to the Second, a shift we have regarded throughout this volume as seismic. In the initial Awakening, Jonathan Edwards calls men and women to faith in Christ on the basis of a rational conviction. He works from a larger system which allows him to interact with the new ideas sweeping Europe. So sophisticated is he in terms of both his grasp of biblical theology and of philosophy that he can even employ John Locke in the service of Christ. Yet, his preaching, though not dramatic or homiletically inspiring, produces enormous emotional effects. The Great Awakening was a rallying cry for supernaturalism in the face of Enlightenment naturalism, but it was hardly antirational or irrational; instead it set out to convert the whole person.

In the Second Awakening, the focus shifts from what God does with humans to what humans do with God. The shift includes a change from theology to sentiment. The goal is not to change the hearers' minds so much as to change their sentiments.

Eventually, the Second Awakening scattered into camp meetings along the sawdust trail. These meetings often reflected a sectarian folk religion comparable to any medieval or modern European sect. "The first jerk or so," wrote frontier preacher Peter Cartwright of early nineteenth-century camp meetings, "you would see their fine bonnets, caps and combs fly; and so sudden would be the jerking of the head that their long loose hair would crack almost as loud as a wagoner's whip." The preachers themselves became hysterical, writhing on the ground in uncommon figures. They "laughed senselessly, 'holy laughs,' they called them." Then "they jumped around like dogs on all fours and, still barking, 'treed the devil' like dogs chasing a squirrel. When all else failed, they spoke in a gibberish which they believed to be the 'other tongues' used by the apostles in the Bible."[5]

This new emotional reaction to rationalistic deism and cold, dead orthodoxy was called the Second Awakening, but it was anything but a successor to the Great Awaken-

ing. It seems, at this point, American individualism per-
sisted. While rationalism insisted that a person could know
all he needs to know through his own reason, the new
revivalism was insisting that a person could know all he
needs to know through his own experience and intuition.
Orthodox Christianity affirmed that, while both reason and
experience are necessary aspects of our faith, revelation
stood as judge over both and dictated the validity of one's
propositions or feelings.

Romanticism

Beginning with Jean-Jacques Rousseau, many of the
brightest children of the rationalistic Enlightenment were
realizing the bankruptcy of a rationalism detached from
transcendent revelation. Convinced of the failure of independent reason to provide the answers to life's greatest
questions, a school of thought known as Romanticism was
born. Romanticism was more committed to intuitive impres-
sions from within than to objective facts from without. The
seeds of Romanticism were sown in the Enlightenment
itself, even though Romanticism was a reaction against
rationalism. Man was good; he just needed absolute freedom and independence from tradition, the past, institutions,
and indeed, society itself. Emerson wrote of "Self-Reliance,"
Wordsworth of coming to realize his own divinity. Of
course, a Romantic way of thinking was already present, as
we have seen, in the intuitive individualism of the frontier.

In his seminal work, *Religion in the Age of Romanticism*,
British historian Bernard Reardon notes that the Romantic
reaction "opposed the abstractions of Newtonian 'reason'
with a new appeal to experience. And the centre of such
experience," Reardon writes, "was of course man himself."[6]
(This man-centeredness is what all of the megatrends shaping American culture share. Reardon comments, "An obvious outcome of this Romantic egotism was an intense emotionalism." Upon further reflection, he adds, "It could more
aptly be described as sentimentalism."[7]) For Romanticism,

for instance, the test of a creed was how it felt—what experiences it engendered. Samuel Taylor Coleridge charged, "Evidences of Christianity! I am weary of the word. Make a man feel the want of it; rouse him if you can, to the self-knowledge of the need for it." After all, "the real evidence of truth," he said, "is in subjectivity." In Novalis's words, "The way to all mysteries heads inwards."

The late eighteenth and early nineteenth centuries saw a birth of new metaphysical, transcendental cults: this, of course, in reaction to the rationalism of the Enlightenment. Quakerism, with its notion of the "divine spark" in every person, grew during this period. For many Quakers, the Bible was not the supreme authority. The "inner light" was authoritative (as reason was for the rationalists) and the sacraments of baptism and communion were jettisoned because they made believers depend too much on the visible, material world outside them.[8] A new sect, the Swedenborgian Church, appeared. It was perhaps the first theosophy (mind science) group in America—a group which would exercise profound influence over thinkers such as Ralph Waldo Emerson.

Transcendentalism

It is difficult to distinguish precisely where Romanticism ends and Transcendentalism begins in the American experience. Emerson, Walt Whitman, Henry David Thoreau, and a host of other writers draw from German Romanticism in their celebration of nature and self.

In Boston, still the intellectual center at this time, Unitarianism was reigning. You will remember that the Unitarian Church was the unofficial state church of Enlightenment deism in America. Jesus was not a divine redeemer, but an enlightened moral example; salvation was not a matter of setting sinners right with God by grace alone, but of social and self-improvement by works. For the Unitarians, Christianity was little more than ethics and inspiration to service.

However, in the 1830s a trend was emerging within Unitarianism which even that group considered heretical: Transcendentalism. As the name suggests, its adherents sought to transcend the physical, tangible, objective world and tap the resources of the spirit. Determined to discover their oneness with the Divine (Emerson's "Over-Soul"), the Transcendentalists were the mystics of their age. Thus, the Boston intelligentsia began moving increasingly from deism to pantheism.

Historian Gregg Singer explains: "Even in those denominations which were historically evangelical . . . , there were strong influences at work for the creation of a 'democratic theology,' namely a theology which would modify such Calvinistic doctrines as the sovereignty of God and the total depravity of the race, in favor of a theology which would emphasize the love of God at the expense of His justice and holiness." Furthermore, this theology "would insist that man was not totally depraved and could, to some degree at least, cooperate with God in the achievement of his own salvation."[9] As Arminianism was a first step toward the democratization of the evangelical faith in America, so Transcendentalism was the radicalization of that process.

Transcendentalism dared to pronounce what Arminianism would never have entertained and which would have caused even polite Unitarians to gasp in horror: the deification of man. Said Emerson, "I see all the currents of the universe being circulated through me; I am a part and parcel of God." This process is clear: From the Puritan belief in human lostness and confidence in the sovereignty of an infinite and yet personal God who was profoundly interested and involved in his creation; to the Arminian weakening of the Protestant view of sin, grace, and divine sovereignty in the interest of human freedom and independence; and then the further weakening of the biblical faith to the level of mere sentiment. Deism entertained a god who was removed from the scene altogether, except as a moral governor and creator. As we reach Transcendentalism, the individual is finally enshrined as the object of knowledge. In the American experience, we come full circle to Satan's first temptation: "You shall be as gods."

Thus, what Friedrich Schlegel called "the abyss of individuality" replaces the sense of being a part of something larger than oneself and subject to a gracious God above. As for the older faith, Emerson informed Harvard in 1838, "There is a great famine in our churches," and argued that "whatever hold the public worship had on men is gone or going." Doubtless, the Bostonian had in mind Unitarianism more than the previous Puritan, evangelical faith. Once the supernaturalism of the Reformation creed was gutted, nothing was left. When God is no longer the center of attention, worship, and religion in general, become rather useless. Without a creed, a tradition, a community, or a philosophy of life, the Transcendentalists turned inward for answers with the intensity with which the Rationalists had turned outward.

One can easily detect how America was engineering its own variety of New Age thought long before the Age of Aquarius, the 1960s. Transcendentalism has parallels in ancient Gnosticism (second century A.D.), in medieval dualism and mysticism, and among the Enthusiasts of the French countryside about the same time as its ascendancy in America.[10] But the rise of mysticism and fascination with the occult during the 1960s was as much an inherently American Transcendentalist phenomenon as an importation from the East. (We will examine the effects of this "New Thought" in the next chapter.) For our purposes, it is enough to make the connection between Romanticism, Transcendentalism, and finally, existentialism.

The purpose for understanding something of all of these movements is to see how our environment has been shaped by successive waves of subjectivism. One can call this subjective tendency in the American personality Romanticism or Transcendentalism or existentialism, depending on what stage or period we are discussing. They are all connected and interdependent. This brings us, then, to the most recent subjectivist movement: existentialism.

Existentialism

A religious impetus gave rise to modern existentialism. As Schleiermacher had turned to Romanticism and pietism (its religious equivalent by this time) in reaction to a similar situation in Germany, so Søren Kierkegaard (1813–1855), despaired of his state church's dead orthodoxy. Kierkegaard, a Danish Lutheran, complained about a religion which had no subjective, experiential aspect; an altogether impractical, unhelpful religion.

Of course, here it is that we, the orthodox, must take our turn at the whipping post. The orthodoxy of the New Testament writers, Luther, and Calvin was anything but cold or dead. The same Luther who shouted at Melanchthon, "The gospel lies entirely outside of you!" and emphasized the objective character of salvation had much to say also about the practical, subjective experience of one's faith. Calvin's rigorous theological discussions are riveting, emotionally charged declarations which speak as much to the heart as to the mind.

Nevertheless, time had passed and the treasures were taken for granted. Heresy was prosecuted, but godliness was not pursued. Truth was maintained, at least on paper, but failed to fuel the heart. Propositions were upheld, while implications were ignored. This loss of a sense of connection between truth and reality, faith and practice, was tragic and produced a world in which religion was irrelevant. Pietism has been characterized as "privately engaging, but socially irrelevant"; dead orthodoxy (against which pietism reacted) was "socially engaging, but privately irrelevant."

So Kierkegaard turned inward. "Truth is subjectivity," he said, not formal propositions which could be defended through reason and evidence. "God is in the creation and present everywhere in it," he asserted, "but directly He is not there; and only when the individual turns to his inner self, and hence only in the inwardness of self-activity, does he have his attention aroused, and is enabled to see God."

Kierkegaard, far from announcing a new philosophical school, merely echoed the words of an anonymous fourteenth-century mystic: "God may be reached by love, but not by thought" (*The Cloud of Unknowing*). Church history is a series of reactions between dogmatism and mysticism. It was Kierkegaard who first suggested that we take the "leap of faith," in spite of the lack of rational answers. This leap becomes the centerpiece of existentialism, both secular and religious. The decision is ultimate, not the objective truth or falsehood of what is believed.

While Kierkegaard was struggling, American revivalists were already preaching a brand of existentialism. With the rejection of Calvinism, according to one historian, "much of modern evangelicalism and fundamentalism tended to shift the focus in Christianity from God's sovereignty to the personal human experience."[11] More and more, evangelists were preaching faith rather than Christ; urging decisions without much knowledge of the nature of what was being decided upon. Not objective truth, but subjective experience, was the focus of such evangelism.

There are also, however, secular roots for existentialism, and we must understand both secular and religious varieties if we are to recognize the extent to which we have been influenced by this movement.

If the Romantics and Transcendentalists reacted against the optimism of the Enlightenment—that all the world's problems could be solved through reason and science—the existentialists reacted against the failure of the Transcendentalists to provide any meaningful answers by looking inward. Existentialists charged both Rationalists and Transcendentalists with a blind and unwarranted optimism.

We have to realize the historical context in which secular existentialism was born. By the end of the nineteenth century, even evangelicals were still confident that the kingdom of God would be established gradually, by the improvement of society. Everybody was optimistic about the future. But then there was the First World War, which, even by modern standards, was a barbaric ground war involving some of the bloodiest battles and indiscriminate slaughter in history.

With the optimism of the Gay '90s tempered, if not

dashed, the new century saw the rise of dictators who were determined to bring the entire world into their own utopia. In 1917, the Bolshevik Revolution turns Russia into the Union of Soviet Socialist Republics, and eventually Joseph Stalin competes with Adolf Hitler for first place in the demonic slaughter of one's own people. Hitler's "utopia" quickly turns into Germany's greatest nightmare and the world's greatest threat.

The existentialists were children of this failed series, cynics about what they perceived as lies Romanticism, Transcendentalism and even scientific rationalism had told them about the goodness and, in fact, perfectability, of human nature. Suddenly, man seemed evil and helpless, unable to save himself, much less the world.

In this respect at least, existentialism was closer to Christianity than the previous movements had been. Nevertheless, though it saw through the illusions, existentialism had no answers to offer in their place. Kierkegaard's leap of faith became, for the secular existentialists, a decision to become "authentic." According to this view, there are two types of people in the world: authentic and synthetic, real and unreal. Those who follow the crowd or the creed are considered synthetic. Their existence is determined by someone outside themselves. They are not "in control." Thus, Jean-Paul Sartre and Albert Camus suggest that the only appropriate response to the human condition is suicide, for it may be the best way of determining one's own fate.

The decline of Christianity, however, had profound influences over even the secular existentialists. For instance, the brutishly anti-Christian, frustrated philosopher, Friedrich Nietzsche (1844–1900), lamented, "Doctrinal Christianity is at an end," and predicted that the West would simply have to settle now for "a reactionary utopia, an 'active nihilism,' a 'new Buddhism.'" This alternative to Christian orthodoxy did not impress Nietzsche. He was not celebrating the "death of God," but hated God all the more because he had "died." But it was Christians themselves who were responsible for killing God: "You have neutered God!" Nietzsche charged the preachers of his day. God was no longer the universal monarch who inspired confidence and awe, but a weak mascot who went along with the crowd.

Nihilism ("meaninglessness" or "nothingness") is a product of existentialism and is usually associated with Nietzsche. "One interpretation of existence," Nietzsche wrote of Christianity, "has been overthrown, but since it was held as *the* interpretation, it seems no meaning is left in existence."[12] Hence, the Russian writer Dmitry Ivanovich Pisarev wrote, prior to the 1917 Revolution, "What can be smashed should be smashed." Marxism-Leninism grew out of this sense of frustration over the meaninglessness of existence, and Nietzsche's two most famous admirers were Lenin and Hitler.

Feodor Dostoevski cautioned, "If God does not exist, everything is permitted." And we have seen that prediction come true again and again in this century. It is easy (and usual) for us to objectify active nihilism as a communist or a Nazi preoccupation, but it grips the free world just as tenaciously.

A number of years ago, before the "wall came tumbling down," I had just returned from East Berlin, a gray, depressing, dull environment. People's spirits seemed damp and defeated. But here I was in the free world again, standing on the steps of the Wilhelm Kirche. With half of its steeple missing and windows blown out, the cathedral stood as a memorial to both the material and the spiritual devastation of the war. On the steps, a group of Hare Krishnas clad in orange gowns sang and passed out tracts. Among them, an intoxicated youth created his own show for the onlookers as he swigged a fifth of whiskey. I was amazed at how nihilism can produce two diverse responses—in the East, resignation; in the West, addiction and diversion. In the East, the state; in the West, drugs and entertainment.

An American existentialist, and a Marxist, Michael Harrington, writes, "Where the Enlightenment had only imagined substitute religions, men and women now tried to create substitute churches," and he speaks regretfully of the "rain of the gods" in America.[13] Even secularists know the truth about our civilization. Our emotional, sentimental religion has knocked the objective, rational foundation from under American Christianity, thereby undermining ultimate meaning for civilization. We have neutered God!

A celebrated historian, Jackson Lears, has characterized the late nineteenth century and the twentieth century as antimodern—a rejection of the industrial manipulation of humans, and a rejection of scientific rationalism and technology in general. Lears notes that "these difficulties were exacerbated by religious changes. As Calvinism softened into platitudinous humanism, Protestant Christianity lost the gravity provided by older, sterner creeds. Lacking spiritual ballast, bourgeois culture entered what Nietzsche called a 'weightless' period." Lears adds that this "weightless" period has been "marked by hazy moral distinctions and vague spiritual commitments." Gradually, "personal identity itself came to seem problematic." In other words, with increasing modernization and urbanization, there was a general loss of the self and its place in this world, since Christianity accommodated to the marketplace instead of offering a challenging alternative.

Lears continues:

> But the trouble ran deeper: the rationalization of urban culture and the *decline of religion into sentimental religiosity* further undermined a solid sense of self . . . A weightless culture of material comfort and spiritual blandness was breeding weightless persons *who longed for intense experience to give some definition*, some distinct outline and substance to their vaporous lives. . . . This newer individualism has been expressed in an upbeat rhetoric of personal liberation [italics added].

The new horizon for antimodernists is, according to Lears, "medieval, Oriental, and other 'primitive' cultures"[14] —just what Nietzsche prophesied. We are even seeing in popular film a rash of movies on the afterlife, incorporating heavy doses of medieval and Oriental mysticism.

With the rejection of Reformation orthodoxy, a faith which, when internalized, gave a person that "solid sense of self" Lears talks about, spiritual ambiguity set in. "Sentimental religiosity" took the place of the Reformed creed, first in evangelicalism and then in the culture generally.

Experiential religion is religion of the moment, not of the lifetime. When the glow wears off, so too does the attraction. Existentialism, then, is an outlook of despair—despair of knowing the objective meaning or truth of things. Therefore, the best we can do is perhaps pretend that there is no meaning or truth and to create our own world of reality in its place. This is the goal of much transcendental, mystical religion. Existentialism is the thinking, honest secularist in confession. Insisting he could find all the answers with nothing more than autonomous reason, the secularist is now giving up on the idea that reason can provide any answers. It is a reckoning with the reality that science, mathematics, philosophy, and technology cannot provide an exhaustive context for the facts. Irrationalism is the only appropriate response to an exhausted and unyielding rationalism: conflicts are due to illusion, and reality cannot be rationally explained. Instead of trying to understand an objective world, create your own!

Closer to Home

We have distinguished between the religious and secular roots of modern existentialism. Now we must turn our attention to the effects these ideas have on our contemporary faith and practice.

First, before the emergence of Romanticism, Transcendentalism, or existentialism, evangelicals were becoming increasingly subjective. For the pietists, Christianity was more an issue of feeling, sentiment, and observing certain legalistic taboos than of believing. Reducing the Christian faith to merely private devotions, private morality, private experience, and so on, pietism was taking evangelical Christianity away from the world and into subjective isolation. The orthodox intellectuals erred by failing to demonstrate the practical relevance of their system; the pietists erred by presuming that genuinely correct feelings and conduct could exist without theological substance. Even today, evangelicals think that experience and morality can be techniqued or legislated without any theological foundation.

Philipp Jacob Spener founded the University of Halle, a college devoted to training in piety and holy living (as that movement defined both), as well as in academic subjects. There was a "genuine fear" among the orthodox clergy (not all of whom were "dead") that such a moralistic and inward-looking approach "would lead to rampant subjectivity and anti-intellectualism."[15] As historian Mark A. Noll notes, "Historians have long studied the relationship between pietism and the Enlightenment. . . . They have noted that pietism and the Enlightenment both attacked Protestant orthodoxy, that both . . . were concerned about practice [morality] more than theory [theology]." Noll concludes, "The crucial historical question is whether pietistic antitraditionalism, individualism, and practicality paved the way for a non-Christian expression of these same traits in the Enlightenment."[16]

Curiously, those who were to eventually overthrow Christendom would be those with pietistic backgrounds. The war would come from the prayer closet, not the classroom, and it would be led by those who insisted that they were pious Christians, not vicious atheists. From Immanuel Kant (1724–1804) to Friedrich Schleiermacher (1768–1834), to Søren Kierkegaard (1813–1855), evangelical pietism paved the way for modern existentialism. While Kant was profound, he was one of the first to relegate religion to the category of non-reason. Further, Kant reasoned that our subjective knowledge is the basis for objective reality, rather than the other way around. With this revolt, argues Harrington, "humans were now creating reality for themselves instead of accepting it as a given from God, and the laws of the mind were being imposed upon the external world, not simply describing it" (p.14). This is almost a textbook definition of existentialism. As for his evangelical faith, Kant insisted, "I had to set limits to knowledge in order to make place for faith," as though too much knowledge might be dangerous for faith.[18]

Kant believed that our minds subjectively interpret the world in such a way that we cannot say we know the world the way it really is. Hence, each person's own mind creates his own perceptions of the world. This viewpoint was a short step from his subjective religious experience, for he had been reared in pietism.

Schleiermacher is known as the father of modern liberalism, and yet he was "educated in Moravian schools where he was deeply impressed by mystical pietism." Not surprisingly, "in 1787 he entered the University of Halle and studied the writings of Kant."[19] According to Schleiermacher, religious feeling, not theological or doctrinal propositions, form the substance of Christianity.

Says Reardon, "Karl Barth was probably right in seeing here the effect of the influence upon Schleiermacher of his Moravian upbringing no less than of the individualistic romanticism into which religious sentiment could so readily be translated. Little wonder that in his eyes theological metaphysics was of slight account, since such argumentation does little to endorse or promote the essentially emotional response in which the religious experience consists."[20]

Thus, modern liberalism in theology was not the result of too much thinking, but of too little! It was not a fair war between rational science and rational, orthodox religion, but between rational science and an anti-intellectual, subjective pietism. This is why we lost the second battle earlier this century. There were too few Warfields and Machens.

The chasm is not wide between the disdain for theology characteristic of modern evangelicals and that which marked the architects of modern secularism. Both have insisted that doctrinal debates are diversions from piety." Both raise their glasses of sentiment in a toast to "Jesus the Person," not "Jesus the Creed." Both champion the existential encounter with Christ in conversion, often quite apart from coming to terms with the historical and theological objectivity of Christ's life and saving work and the social dimensions of the faith in this world. The Bible may be inaccurate about history and science, but "its integrity is not seriously undermined," because the religion is about one's own existential encounters with Christ, not with things which happened two thousand years ago. So the reasoning goes.

Martin E. Marty observes the following:

> In contemporary America, one might almost note that the seminaries devoted to heart religion are well-supported, while those that deal with theology suffer. The institutes that bring religious people together find themselves regularly devoted to experience. Theology is not a prime topic at most. They become preoccupied with the human potential movement, bodily awareness, celebration, spiritual experiences—all of them legitimate, but not by themselves the whole show of Christian life.
>
> Sermons are used for inspiring without informing, and are often an embarassment to thoughtful people—most of whom eventually stay away. . . . In religious publishing, people pay for every kind of book about how one experienced Jesus or the Holy Spirit, but first-rate books about how one might think about them go neglected.[21]

Not only did we miss our opportunity to "give to every man an answer" at a time when many were asking; but also we failed to appreciate the richness of our biblical faith even for ourselves. Marty argues, "Those who make so much of experiences such as conversion or enlightenment and play down all attempts to connect these to ways of life or ways of looking at the world overlook too much of biblical revelation. When the anti-intellectual American Christian criticizes anyone who wants to see what the faith has to do with philosophy, politics, or other human enterprises, he overlooks the kind of material presented in the first chapter of Paul's letter to the Colossians. There," Marty says, "Jesus Christ is described as the one for whom and in whom and through whom all things are created and in whom 'all things hold together.'"[22] British thinker Harry Blamires struggles for words when he laments, "It is difficult to do justice . . . to the complete loss of intellectual morale in the twentieth-century Church."[23]

Finally, Marty compares contemporary evangelicals to earlier Christians: "Whereas early Christian fathers, medieval leaders, Reformation figures had all 'argued' and constructed patterns of thought by which to address the new situations, in the new era people stopped arguing. According to Alfred North Whitehead, it was a fateful moment when the clergy of the Western world stopped appealing to constructive reason to set forth the place of their faith and experience." Consequently, "the modern world grew up progressively independent of religious norms."[24]

Marty is not alone in this assessment. Harvey Cox concurs:

> Now not only was theology incompetent and uninterested in politics, science, technology, and the rest, so was God. These fields, the faithful were assured, were autonomous realms with their own built-in self-guiding mechanisms. . . . Now God, maker of heaven and earth, became the deity of religion, approached through what came to be called "religious experiences." Modern religion was born. A faith that had once proclaimed a Lord who lifted up and cast down emperors, who condemned extortion and profit gouging, was now reduced to being concerned exclusively with the inner spirit.[25]

Eventually, the meaning Christianity had provided for all of life—its profound explanations of work, social relations, tradition, family, freedom, duty, individual, community—evaporated. And nothing was left but "active nihilism or a new Buddhism" (Nietzsche).

According to Noll, Nathan Hatch, and George Marsden, "The faith of evangelicals—internal, private, perfectionistic, individualistic—denied the public, social, realistic, and com-

munal aspects of Puritan Christianity. Ironically, by the
Puritan standard, American evangelicalism itself contributed to the destruction of positive Christian influences
in America, a fact that evangelical spokespersons themselves so much lament."[26] It is, therefore, not secular
humanists who are to blame, but we ourselves, for the loss
of the "older, sterner creed" which Lears insists "provided
spiritual ballast," in whose absence we are left with "weightless souls."

Karl Marx himself announced that "the holy shudder of
pious ecstasy . . . had been drowned in the ice-cold water of
egotistical calculation. . . . All fixed and deeply rooted relations, with their train of venerable images and world-views,
were dissolved."[27] No wonder that Marx, surrounded by
German pietism, could regard religion as a drug, "the opiate
of the people."

Conclusion

The non-Christian has no right to believe in reason, but he
does. Nevertheless, revelation-denying rationalism always
ends in irrationalism. Once we have enough time to realize
the failed promises of rationalistic "enlightenment," we
rightly become cynical.

Christianity provides a comfortable home for reason and
revelation. It is a faith that is not afraid of testing its claims
by the use of reason, logic, or evidences, but which, in fact,
appeals to those very sources for support. And yet, we all
know the limits of reason. That is where revelation enters.

Reason, according to revelation (Rom. 1), can learn that
God exists and can even know certain things about God.
But it cannot know that he is a Trinity; that he wants to
relate personally to his creatures, and that he has sent his
Son to save the world from guilt and sins. That is vital
information, yet it cannot be learned by reason alone.
Christianity is not antirational, irrational, or nonrational,
but it transcends reason. It provides answers which observable data cannot verify. And yet, because reason and evi-

dence have been shown to support revelation's truth claims, we learn to make that transition from reason alone to revelation. This is how we actually preserve reason, how we keep from despairing of ever understanding the meaning of it all. We put reason and revelation together and we find harmony—tension, from time to time, but an equilibrium. At last, "reasonable faith" is not an oxymoron.

If there is one thing we learn from Solomon's wisdom, it is that false gods, when worshiped, become demons. Moralism undermined morality; legalism, law; rationalism, reason; mysticism, mystery; pietism, piety. If we learn from the past and untangle ourselves from its irrationalism, we can meet the culture with the Christian challenge at an opportune moment. Existential philosopher Colin Wilson writes, "Existentialism has reached a standstill. . . . Man is free, but the world is empty and meaningless—this is the problem. While this sentence remains a summary of existentialism, there is nothing further to be done."[28] With the refreshing honesty characteristic of existentialism, Wilson shows us here the open door. Nothing is replacing existentialism and yet existentialism itself recognizes that it is a vacuum waiting to be filled.

At present, our culture is sliding into a new Dark Age of superstition and ignorance. Evangelicals can do nothing about it unless they are themselves committed to understanding what they believe and why they believe it. We must stop mimicking the world in its search for self-actualization, the inner self, and other forms of narcissism.

At the same time Napoleon Bonaparte made his concordat with Rome, Chateaubriand wrote, "There was a need for faith, a desire for religious consolation, which came from the very lack of that consolation for so many years. People," he said, "hurried to the house of God." We have seen the famine. Let us prepare the feast.

The Return to Paganism 6

I predict that in our lifetime we will see a New World Religion. . . . I believe a new spiritual system will emerge.
—Jean Houston, Association for Humanistic Psychology

Having done with the sovereign God whose glory is the goal of human existence, Enlightenment secularism only returned the culture to paganism. Leszek Kolakowski spoke of "a rain of Gods . . . falling from the sky on the funeral rites of the one God who has outlived himself."[1] "The West," notes Michael Harrington, "has raised up an entire pantheon to blot out the emptiness of its heavens."[2] Just when the supposed death of the traditional God was being mourned, new gods were waiting in the wings: nation, race, materialism, totalitarianism, and the state.

The nineties must represent the decade of magic. Lucifer has been getting a lot of attention these days, whether in popular literature and film (both Christian and secular) or in the occult. Nevertheless, here, too, Christians must beware. Fascination with the devil (humans have always had a love-hate relationship with him) can become a superstitious medieval preoccupation when we seek to interpret everything in the natural world as a struggle between the forces of good and evil.

So many studies of the New Age movement are available that I hardly expect to throw great beams of light on the subject, but I do think it is a logical progression of subjectivism and has affected the evangelical community in ironic and important ways. This should not be surprising. As we have seen, when the world was calling for a positive mental attitude, self-fulfillment, and health, wealth, and happiness, we invented gospels suited to their sensitivities. It should not come as a surprise, then, that contemporary evangelicalism has accommodated in significant ways to the spirit of the age—of the New Age, that is.

Although the New Age movement has gained considerable publicity and attention in bookstores and in entertainment, its adherents, according to one estimate, number no more than twenty thousand. We may have reason to dismiss it as a passing fad, but it is important to note that many of the movement's adherents are prominent leaders in influential fields. Rather that inspiring paranoia, this should lead us to ask, "What is it about the failure of scientific rationalism that makes even well-educated philosophers, scientists, and educators move in this direction?" the New Age movement as an entity may not be as significant as its zealous critics have suggested, but it does point up a deep current of mysticism and antirationalism flowing beneath the surface of modern discourse.

The Roots of the New Age Movement

It is often supposed that the origin of the New Age movement lies in the importation of Eastern religion during the 1960s. But as we have seen, America has had its own metaphysical superstition for some time. Theosophical speculation became an important pastime for many of the Transcendentalists of the last century. Let's explore these roots more closely.

Theosophy

"All theosophical speculation," according to the *Encyclopaedia Britannica,* "is based on the mystical premise that God must be experienced directly to be known at all." (This, of course, is the same rationale employed by medieval mystics who sought a direct, immediate, intuitive encounter with God. They sought to see and touch the "naked God," as Martin Luther, a critic of the "ladder of mysticism," put it.) A Russian-born mystic, Helena Blavatsky, founded the Theosophical Society in 1875.

Encyclopaedia Britannica tells us that theosophy refers "to a certain strain of mystical thought to be found in such thinkers as the ancient Greek philosophers Pythagoras and Plato; the Gnostic teachers Simon Magus and Valentinus; the Neoplatonist philosophers Plotinus and Proclus; the medieval northern European mystics Meister Eckhardt and Nicholas of Cusa; the Renaissance speculative mystics Paracelsus and Giordano Bruno; the German philosophical mystic Jakob Boehme; and the German Romantic philosopher Friedrich Schelling. But," the *Encyclopaedia* concludes, "the richest and most profound source of theosophical views has been Indian thought, where it may be traced from the earliest Vedas (Hindu scriptures) to modern times." It should be noted that it was Gnosticism and Greek metaphysics which the New Testament and early church so resolutely opposed.

Dualism

All of these movements have one thing in common: they are "dualistic," that is, they divide the world into "good" and "bad," which usually means "spiritual" and "material." In Zoroastrianism, for instance, a good god and a bad god struggle for dominance. Eastern religions are also heavily influenced by this dualistic preoccupation with demons and the spirit world. In Christianity, of course, there is a real, personal devil, but the devil is not a "bad god." Even the devil is under divine authority and God himself decides when and where evil will be allowed in order to fulfill a larger purpose. While Christianity recognizes the struggle with "powers and principalities in heavenly places," it does not make this warfare central in its theology. Rather than seeing the problem of sin and suffering in terms of a war between the good god and bad god, Christians see the problem in terms of sin and grace. Nature is not evil; matter is real and created by God to be enjoyed and cared for.

Active Nihilism and New Buddhism

You will remember from chapter 6 Friedrich Nietzsche's prediction that the decline of "doctrinal Christianity" would produce an era of "active nihilism and a new Buddhism." We saw active nihilism in the Second World War and are now faced with the new Buddhism.

Now we have the New Age movement, the Age of Aquarius. The inner journey of mystical experience is not merely the eccentric hobby of Hollywood movie stars, airport solicitors clad in colorful draperies, and residents of California's Marin County. In the largest bookstore chains, the New Age section dominates half the store. Books in other sections (especially psychology) push their subject matter to the edges of the New Age movement in order to appeal to a mass-market audience.

How Extensive Is the Movement?

During the Middle Ages, science was often indistinguishable from superstition, in which alchemy and astrology reigned. Of course, our technological sophistication has increased, but is it possible that our intellectual, philosophical, and moral outlook is returning to the Dark Ages?

Even within the scientific community people are trading their scientific rationalism for superstitions. Scientists from Stanford University to Cambridge (including a Nobel Prize-winner in physics, Brian Josephson) are embracing New Age thought as the guiding light of what they unabashedly call science.[3]

Medicine, business, psychology, entertainment, government, and education are now tinkering with or adopting New Age concepts. It has become dangerous, in fact, in intellectual circles, to condemn mysticism. The intelligensia seems to be so attracted to an anti-materialistic, antirational or, at best, suprarational outlook, that one can more easily contest rationalism than mysticism these days. Having done with revelation, Western culture has given up on reason as well.

It is important, then, that we realize that mysticism is no longer the hobby of a few eccentrics. Superstition captivates the imaginations of many of the new thinkers, whether scientists, historians, economists, politicians, educators, or religionists. The hippies of the 1960s have become the yuppies of the 1990s and many have brought their Transcendentalism with them. Stories which would once be confined to the *National Enquirer* are now printed in *Omni, Psychology Today, Discover*, and other popular scientific periodicals.

The *New York Times* ran a story in September 1987, concerning a New Age conference: "Representatives of some of the nation's largest corporations, including I.B.M., A.T. & T., and General Motors, met in New Mexico in July to discuss how metaphysics, the occult, and Hindu mysticism might help executives compete in the world marketplace." The *Times* writer added, "New Age thought . . . rejects the Judeo-Christian concept of a single, omnipotent God Who has revealed His will to man. Instead, New Age adherents follow the view of many Eastern religions that there is a unity in the universe, of which all things, including God and man, are equal parts."

Thus, according to this view, "man himself is a deity who can 'create his own reality.'" (This, you will remember, was the hallmark of Transcendentalism.) The *New York Times* article further stated that in these sessions in which employees are hypnotized, "one concept commonly transmitted . . . is that because man is a deity equal to God he can do no wrong; thus, there is no sin, no reason for guilt in this life." This revealing article referred to such institutions as "Stanford University's well-regarded Graduate School of Business" where students are issued "a syllabus for a seminar on 'Creativity in Business'" which includes "meditation, chanting, 'dream work,' the use of tarot cards and discussion of the 'New Age Capitalist.'"

In what is called the "handbook of the New Age movement," Marilyn Ferguson states, "Like that of the founding fathers and of the American Transcendentalists of the mid-1800s, the dream of the Aquarian Conspiracy in America is a framework for nonmaterialist expansion: autonomy, awakening, creativity—and reconciliation."[4] The movement, she says, is "reluctant to create hierarchical structures" and is "averse to dogma. And perhaps, by integrating magic and science, art and technology, it will succeed where all the king's horses and all the king's men have failed."[5]

But no more tragic is the seduction, as some have called it, than in religion, particularly in evangelicalism. Now we must tread carefully here. There has been a good deal of witch-hunting and conspiracy-probing. Many well-meaning Christians look for New Age influences and seductions under every rock. Someone uses a term that New Agers use and suddenly he or she is put out on a limb with Shirley. That is, of course, irresponsible. Nonetheless, that must not distract us from the influences a vast movement is bound to have even on those of us who think we are immune to it.

After a number of rounds (from Arminianism to deism to Unitarianism to Romanticism to Transcendentalism to existentialism to the New Age explosion), we have suffered successive blows to the Christian faith. We helped, by watering the message down in an effort to accommodate rather than to challenge the culture. We thought it would help reach people, but instead, it looked like a cheap imitation of what they had.

With Arminianism, for example, there was what the nation's first evangelicals would have considered a major compromise, a shift from God to man. With each new wave, that man-centeredness intensifies until we see Shirley McLaine in a television movie shouting, "I am God, I am

God." And yet, many televangelists, passing themselves off as evangelicals, say the same thing. "You're not partly God," evangelist Kenneth Copeland informs us, "You're all God. . . . You don't have a god living *in* you; you *are* one!"[6] Similarly, when Sun Myung Moon, founder of the Unification Church, tells his followers that "man is incarnate God," it is no less than television evangelist Kenneth Hagin, a favorite of Christian radio, who tells us, "The believer is as much an incarnation of God as Jesus Christ."[7]

Nevertheless, it is dangerous to criticize such preachers on the basis of their theology, since they get results and provide so many with meaningful spiritual experiences. Here pragmatism and consumerism come into play, along with the other factors we've discussed. After editing *The Agony of Deceit* and defending its charges of heresy against many of these televangelists, I am an expert on the evangelical response to heresy. I must admit that, after dozens of radio and television appearances, I am more worried about the evangelical faith in this country than ever. If you think the New Age rage is simply a passing Hollywood phenomenon, I think time will tell the opposite. I wonder whether evangelical Christianity can survive another era of being "tossed back and forth with every wind of doctrine," whether the ideas are from the East, or from Transcendentalism, or a strange new philosophy from some other part of the globe.

Sociologist Christopher Lasch put it this way: "Since 'the society' has no future, it makes sense to . . . fix our eyes on our own 'private performance,' to become connoisseurs of our own decadence, to cultivate a 'transcendental self-attention,'"[8] and many evangelicals appear to be doing as well at this as non-Christians. Peter Marin adds, "The world view emerging among us centers solely on the self and has individual survival as its sole good."[9]

Anything that leads to a psychic Xanadu is permissible. During the 1960s and 1970s, psychedelic drugs played a significant role in helping people toward "self-realization" and transcendence. Today one in six working adults is addicted to narcotics.

The church, however, must respond to the crisis of truth and meaning differently. The fascination evangelical communicators seem to have with the inner self, with techniques for living the "Higher Life" (the Keswick movement), with steps for attaining direct encounters with God, must be contested as sub-biblical and sub-Christian.

We are often surprised to discover the amount of mystical, subjective speculation in our own thinking. In popular hymnody, for instance, a little sentimentalism creeps in with the explanation for Christianity—"You ask me how I know He lives? He lives within my heart"—and speaks as if we "walked with Him and talked with Him" in a garden. Tim Stafford wrote *Knowing the Face of God* a few years ago, and in an interview he stated, "We sing, 'He Touched Me,' but He really doesn't. If He did, we'd probably turn into ash." Nevertheless, God does maintain his holy, transcendent presence among us in his providence, in his Word, and in his sacraments. He has sent us his Holy Spirit to indwell us, referring to us as "temples" of his presence. But notice, this is done through means appointed by God. It is not through a technique or a direct encounter with God, but through a book, through wine, bread, and water which he has ordained for our communion with him.

As the evangelical Keswick movement calls Christians to "Higher Life," so the New Age movement calls us to aspire to "Higher Consciousness." Princeton's defender of the faith toward the end of the last century, B. B. Warfield, saw the mystical, theosophical influences in the Keswick meetings, and we can see the same dualistic anthropology in Dallas Seminary's founder, Lewis Sperry Chafer, as we see in medieval and Transcendental mysticism.[10]

Even earlier, we can see parallels between pietism and mysticism. In fact, it is the New Age spokesperson, Marilyn Ferguson herself, who includes pietists in her history of the Aquarian Conspiracy: "At first the traditions were transmitted intimately, by medieval alchemists, Gnostics, cabalists, and hermetics. . . . Among the bold and isolated voices were Meister Eckhart, Jakob Boehme [a German pietist], . . .

Emmanuel Swedenborg" (the Swedish-born pietist who, after "conversing with angels," founded a sect in America to which Emerson and Thoreau looked for guidance). Further, "The Transcendentalists . . . rebelled against what seemed the dead, dry intellectualism of the day."[11]

This same New Age representative memorializes the day "in 1902" when "William James . . . redefined religion not as doctrine but as experience."[12] One wonders to what extent today's evangelicals, too, would immortalize that day.

Spiritual Technology

Add to pragmatism and consumerism a generous dose of self-fulfillment programs and subjectivism and the result is what sociologists Louis Schneider and Sanford M. Dornbusch call "spiritual technology."[13] As Georgia Harkness noted, there is a difference between "glorifying God, which is religion and using God, which is magic."[14]

As Ferguson reported, the New Age movement promises to blend science and magic. To that, some evangelicals have merely thrown in a dash of religion. For instance, Pat Robertson writes, "Spirit controls matter. . . . The mind is the ultimate conduit of the spirit. In other words," he says, "when you confess blessing, favor, victory, and success, those things will come to you."[15] Further, those who remain ill or poverty-stricken demonstrate they have "failed to grasp the points we have been making" or are "not living according to the major principles" which Robertson refers to as "laws of prosperity."[16] Just as surely as scientific laws, these spiritual laws govern good or ill fortune. God's name is "like a blank check," the evangelist adds.[17] "Use the water in the reservoir. Remember that faith is the title deed to that pool of power. It is all ours if we know *the rules of miracles*."[18]

This sort of talk abounds in neo-Pentecostal circles, and it is difficult at times to distinguish where Pentecostalism ends and New Age superstition begins in such groups. Both, it seems, are so preoccupied with the realm of the spirit that the charge of a sub-Christian, dualistic, heretical mysticism is hardly more out of place for one than for the other. For this is magic—"spiritual technology," the blending of pseudo-science with pseudo-religion. Its chief end is not to glorify but to use God in self-interest.

Another aspect of this spiritual technology is the promise of creating one's own reality, a concern paramount for the Transcendentalists. Henry David Thoreau wrote, "Not till we are lost, in other words, not till we have lost the world, do we begin to find ourselves, and realize where we are and the infinite extent of our relations."[19] Knowledge does not come by understanding the real world objectively, "but in flashes of light from heaven."[20] Thus, the invitation to "explore your own higher altitudes. . . . Nay be a Columbus to whole new continents and worlds within you, opening new channels. . . . Every man is the lord of a realm beside which the earthly empire of the Czar is but a petty state."[21] Hence, "you conquer fate by thought."[22] "Mind over matter" became a hallmark of the mind-science cults which grew out of Transcendentalism.

As Transcendentalism gave way to "New Thought," with its many metaphysical varieties—Christian Science, Religious Science, the Unity School, and numerous smaller sects—even more traditional groups were affected. It was through Ralph Waldo Trine, an adherent of Christian Science, that E. W. Kenyon discovered theosophy, as it had come to be called. Kenyon is the father of the "faith movement," represented by Copeland, Hagin, Fred Price, Oral Roberts, Paul Crouch, the Rhema Bible Institute, the Trinity Broadcasting Network, and numerous publishing and media ministries. Thus, a direct line can be traced from the nineteenth-century metaphysical, theosophical cults and the contemporary neo-Pentecostal movement.[23]

As for the content, the spiritual technology to which we referred, the emphasis in neo-Pentecostalism on creating reality is surely as strong as anything Emerson or Thoreau ever imagined. For instance, Paul Yonggi Cho, the pastor of the world's largest church (Seoul's Full Gospel Church) gives us this explanation of how a Christian can create his own reality: "God spoke to my heart, 'Son . . . the fourth dimension includes and controls the third dimension. . . . You may wonder how we can *incubate our subconscious* . . . . The only way for us to incubate is through our imagina- tions. . . . Through *visualizing and dreaming* you can incubate your future and hatch the results."[24] This sounds like a Spielberg or a Lucas film! Hi-tech terminology and concepts meet a warped, primitive, superstitious religion of magic. God himself is at the bidding of the believer: "You create the presence of Jesus with your mouth. . . . He is bound by your lips and by your words."[25]

In his introduction to Cho's *Fourth Dimension*, Robert Schuller comments, "You don't know what power you have within you! . . . You make the world into anything you choose. Yes, you can make your world into whatever you want it to be." New Age Transcendentalism has brought together Pentecostals, mainline liberals and evangelicals, nondenominational Christians, Mormons, and Roman Cath- olics as these groups begin embracing the human potential movement. No wonder mainline churchman Norman Vincent Peale could tell an audience on "Donahue," "I know a Shinto temple in Japan where I found eternal peace one day in my soul," while charismatic leader Earl Paulk says, "For years we have said the Mormons are wrong and they have to change. . . . Well, maybe we're the ones who have to change."[26]

Donald G. Bloesch correctly predicted that "the spirituali- ty of the new age will have more kinship with Gnosticism and the ancient mystery religions than with either deism or scientism, the credos of the Enlightenment."[27]

At Unity Village, Schuller answered a question about the "role of what you might consider the New Age minister, in the eighties and beyond." His answer: "We have to posi- tivize religion," in contrast to the older creed that "uses words like sin, salvation, repentance, guilt, that sort of thing."[28] And Dr. David Stoop, on staff at an evangelical megachurch in Newport Beach, California, writes in *Self- Talk*, "The power released by our Self-Talk is incredible. Not

only do our thoughts and words create our emotions, they
have the power to make us well or sick, and to determine
our future."[29] Of course, this is the creed of Christian Science
—mind over matter.

Bloesch warns, "Religion and prayer become reduced to
techniques that facilitate self-realization. . . . Spiritual
progress charts and prayer chains play an important role in
this enterprise. Faith healing becomes less an act of faith
than a technique to bend the will of God. When the age of
technocracy, which paradoxically is the age of Aquarius,
becomes the age of Armageddon, mysticism will begin to
shed its scientific trappings and become a servant of the will
to power."[30] Whether that ominous prediction is likely to be
fulfilled lies outside the scope of our discussion; nevertheless, the point is worth considering.

Pat Robertson not only embraces the "mind over matter"
philosophy of Transcendentalism, but denies the reality of
matter altogether: "Matter is merely a form of energy. The
great paradox is that what we perceive as real and tangible
is actually an illusion. The reality is energy."[31] This is all in
keeping with the emerging world view of what has been
called "the new paganism."

Princeton's B. B. Warfield, perhaps the most articulate
and erudite defender of orthodoxy since Jonathan Edwards,
wrote almost a century ago of the dangers of repeating the
past. As he saw the influence of Transcendentalism on even
mainstream Christianity during his own time, he found
cause for cautioning, "The results which were reached by
the Mystics under the guiding impulse of religious feeling
have in our days been attained in the way of speculation,
thought and meditation. The unity of the divine and human,
of God and man, is the conclusion at which modern speculation in the hands of Hegel and Schelling has arrived."[32]

Process Theism

Hegel and Schelling were also instrumental in construct-
ing a system which would produce process thought. Perhaps

the most popular philosophical and theological fashion today, process philosophy imagines a god who, like George Burns in *Oh, God!* is finite and, in many ways, as much a part of creation as we ourselves. (Another popular manifestation of this outlook is Rabbi Harold Kushner's *When Bad Things Happen to Good People.)* God is "becoming" along with us, coming to greater self-realization through his interaction with humans. Always changing, God is able to relate to our problems as a partner instead of as an aloof monarch. God does not even know the future, according to process theism, so how can he predict, much less control, the destinies of men and nations?

Of course, this is not the God Christians have worshiped. It is not even theism (belief in God), as understood by the world's three major religions. And yet, it is now embraced and promoted not only by postmodern liberals, but also by some leading evangelical thinkers. And it is gaining quite a hearing.

For instance, Richard Rice tells us that God experiences time and events just like we do. He is surprised and even caught off guard. "This also means that not even God knows the future in all its details."[33] But does Rice inform us that he is making a break with classical Christianity? Hardly! Instead, he announces that "our fundamental perspective is that of conservative Christianity."[34] And at least one evangelical publisher believed him. Further, Rice insists that God is not perfect, and that he changes. This must be in order for man to have the freedom he requires. And the architects of process philosophy (Alfred North Whitehead, Charles Hartshorne, John B. Cobb, Jr., John Hick) are freely quoted as authorities.[35]

Clark Pinnock, one of evangelicalism's leading thinkers, has embraced this concept of God as well. In November 1990, Christians United for Reformation sponsored a conference with Rice, Pinnock, and Robert Webber from Wheaton College. Our subject was a megashift in evangelical theology from an "old model," focusing on God's sovereignty and human helplessness, the need for redemption and grace; to a "new model," focusing on man's freedom and goodness and the need for a moral example or crusader against demonic forces. This megashift was first noted in an article in *Christianity Today*. Many evangelical leaders share a sense that some shift has taken place, and while most of those who might defend the shift to a new model would not embrace process theism in all its details, the shrinking concept of God and emphasis on human potential within evangelicalism generally reflects the same intellectual directions.

A church historian at Gordon-Conwell, David F. Wells, says, "I cannot see it all surviving." In fact, he warns, "That a sundering of the movement is coming seems utterly certain to me; the only question is when, how, and with what consequences."[36] This latest shift from a God-centered to a human-centered outlook may test the limits of the label *evangelical*.

Meanwhile, this is not what the world needs . . . or wants! In an effort to be relevant, we create a god only to be told by the masses, *Your God Is Too Small*.

The New Age Rage: Characteristics and Effects

We do have to be careful in making everything from psychology to process philosophy subheadings under New Age. In fact, there might be more wisdom in seeing the New Age movement as nothing more than a symptom of a much deeper and lasting paganism. As we move progressively from a high doctrine of God to a considerably lower view, ecularization is inevitable. And once a society moves beyond secularization, it returns to pre-Christian paganism. The New Age movement may be short-lived, but the world view which spawned it is bound to continue shaping and molding us.

To that end, we should observe the chief characteristics of the movement and point out any inroads each distinctive may have made in mainstream evangelicalism.

Individualism

Anything distinctively American will be distinctively individualistic. This is one reason why it is difficult to define exactly the New Age movement. Its sectarianism is promoted by its insistence on individuality and self-realization. The New Age, in taking the individual from autonomous reason to autonomous experience, has as its goal the authentication and affirmation of the self.

The movement has to compensate for the loss of tradition and community by offering encounter groups and psychotherapy. Touching, caring, relating—these all become techniques we must learn, since we are losing the spontaneity of simple relationships. The movement promises a restoration of human dignity, but insists that "the human brain and behavior are almost unbelievably plastic"[37] and thus undermines the spirituality of being human with a scientific materialism which the movement insists it repudiates. Such inconsistencies abound.

Applied to the business world, mystical self-preoccupation merely reinvigorates the self-centered philosophy of the past decades. "From the Zen viewpoint," according to guru Roshi Kapleau, in a conversation with a student, "work has a far deeper purpose than simply turning out a product or rendering a service useful to society. Rightly regarded, it is a vehicle for Self-realization. . . . To work this way is called in Zen working for oneself." The student responded, "Working for yourself while working for the company—that should make everybody happy."[38] What a contrast with the Protestant work ethic, in which producing a quality product and being given by God himself a gift to use in the service of the community and God's glory is the object! How different is the Zen self-centeredness from the culture of narcissism?

And yet, Christian churches must pause to ask why those young people, many of whom were reared in church-going families, failed to find genuine community and fellowship in the church. We should neither sacrifice authentic fellowship nor indulge in what some call "koinoniaitis." Fellowship cannot be treated as an end in itself, but rather as a means of growth in grace. In church, at school, at work, in hospitals, in communities, and in prisons, Christians must be recognized as people who treat everybody with the dignity that being created in God's image deserves. We have to be more interested in people than in numbers.

Furthermore, therapeutic "fellowship" that is techniqued and programed in small groups cannot take the place of friendship. We need to be better friends—especially to non-Christians in our past who may have felt that we saw them as souls to be won. "It's just not the same between us," some of these people have said to friends who have become believers. It may never be the same, but we have to be better friends than we sometimes are.

No church program, evangelistic meeting, or small group can do what honest, spontaneous friendships do. Although the New Agers are individualistic, they do crave community (as the cults demonstrate). The church can provide a sense of true community—not "sloppy agape" or false smiles, but real discipleship and friendship.

Gnosticism

Passing references have been made to this early sect. Known particularly for its dualist view of good and evil, light and darkness, spirit and matter, Gnosticism was the greatest threat to the orthodoxy and stability of the early church. In fact, it is postulated that most of the New Testament epistles combat this blend of Greek mystery religion, Persian and Oriental mysticism, and Christianity.

This dualistic outlook has resurfaced throughout church history, in the form of what is often called neo-Platonism. The spirituality of medieval mystics as well as heretical medieval sects was shaped by this dualistic view. All of life is viewed as a war between the forces of good (angels) and bad (demons). The medieval world, with its superstition, was heavily saturated with this other-worldly speculation. It was difficult, at times, to discern the point at which ritual turned into magic and religion was transformed into the occult.

The Reformation, in many ways, was a reaction against superstition and magic and a call to recover a reasonable faith. Leaving off images, the Reformers argued, Christians should become people of the book again. But, as we saw earlier, less than three centuries later frontier evangelicalism became increasingly dualistic and mystical, focusing on the inner spirit rather than on the historical Christ. Finally, Transcendentalism revived an outright Gnostic gospel. "Don't focus on that body of yours," evangelist Kenneth Copeland tells his modern American audiences, in true Gnostic fashion. In *The Reflexive Universe,* New Ager Arthur Young argues, "We represent a 'fall' into matter from light, and the lightward ascent has begun again."[39]

The body, matter, knowledge that comes through study and books, tradition, creeds, doctrines—these are all bound to imprison the spirit, the Gnostics have argued. Instead of understanding the world as it is, we are to create a spiritual reality; rather than following Saint Paul's command to "do your best to present yourself to God as one approved, a workman who does not need to be ashamed" (2 Tim. 2:15), the believer ought to open himself up to direct intuitive revelations. Thus, Gnosticism is intrinsically anti-intellectual.

Ferguson, in promoting the New Age, writes, "It is not more knowledge, but a new way of knowing" (p. 30). Similarly, televangelist Copeland says, "The problem area is not in your spirit; it lies in your mind and body."[41] Consequently, according to Kenneth Hagin, the believer ought not to trust his mind: "The mind will trip you up and cause you to fall," he tells his television audiences.

The New Age movement proudly points to Gnosticism as an antecedent. Eric Voegelin, director of the Institute for Political Science at the University of Munich, argues in *Science, Politics, and Gnosticism* that "the world is no longer the . . . Judeo-Christian world that God created and found good. Gnostic man no longer wishes to perceive in admiration the intrinsic order of the cosmos. For him the world has become a prison from which he wants to escape." There is one universal dogma of Gnosticism, he writes: "The experience of a world as an alien place into which man has strayed and from which he must find his way back home to the other world of his origin."[42]

This, curiously, is the tendency not only of mystics, but also of mainstream American evangelicalism. Historically, the doctrine of creation gave Christians the confidence that this world and this life are important. God had created us, given us callings, and provided means for taking pleasure in the things he created for the purpose of reflecting on his goodness. This is an important aspect of spirituality for Luther, Calvin, and the Puritans. But moderns, Christians and non-Christians, seem to be anti-worldly and suspicious of the intellect, the body, sacraments, tradition, ritual, doctrine, creeds, and anything that is too human or physical. Ironically, these same people often endorse a materialistic, hedonistic way of life that contradicts their other-worldly rhetoric.

It is ironic that Gnostics would be interested in the environment, but many New Agers are indeed. One would think that a disdain for matter and an obsession with spirit would at the least produce a lack of interest in preserving the physical environment from which we should seek to escape. Nevertheless, consistent or not, New Age adherents have often done more than Christians in such causes.

As we think of how we might be better witnesses to these who have become cynical about the relevance of Christianity, we ought to demonstrate with our hands that it is the Judeo-Christian tradition which says God created matter good, and that the world is fallen—not from spirit to matter, but from obedience to rebellion. Even in redemption, God has in mind not only souls but also bodies and, in fact, the entire created order: "The creation itself will be liberated from its bondage to decay and brought into the glorious freedom of the children of God" (Rom. 8:21). The physical environment should be a concern for Christians far more than for Gnostics.

Positive Mental Attitude

Werner Erhardt, the founder of est, calls it "positive mental attitude"; Peale and Schuller call it "positive thinking"; the neo-Pentecostals call it "positive confession." But whatever one calls it, there is one dogma with which modern American religion will not part: optimism.

This, too, is part of the hedonism of our time. Many people today simply do not want to hear bad news; they do not want to be disturbed. Historic Christianity maintains a realism which avoids the extremes of existential despair and Romantic or Transcendental optimism. The sorrow and wrongs in the world have an explanation: humans are born in original sin, shaped in corruption by virtue of their solidarity with Adam. Humans cannot build a perfect world. And yet, God is sovereign and has everything under control. He can be trusted for salvation and for improvement of individuals and societies, but by grace, not by manipulation or technique. Nevertheless, modern religion has replaced a weak creature with a weak Creator. Instead of making himself an equal of an almighty God, modern humans have made a god as weak as themselves.

Optimism about human potential will always disappoint, but God is a constant. If we seek to become like God (Satan's ever-popular lie), we will bring him down to our smallness instead of rising to his greatness. Our idols will be only as great as the noblest man or woman.

But we must tell the truth. There is much that is negative in Christianity. But if there weren't, Christianity would not be a realistic religion—negative things are part of the real world. The Bible simply explains the situation the way it really is, warts and all.

Therapeutic Well-Being

The New Age is addicted to psychological therapies. This is due, in part, to the preoccupation with self. During the 1960s and 1970s, drugs were supposed to put people in touch with their inner selves. In the 1980s and 1990s, therapy is supposed to promote self-realization.

The world-renowned psychologist Viktor Frankl noted by the end of the 1960s that "a psychiatrist today is confronted more and more with a new type of patient, a new class of neurosis." No longer, he argues, is psychology concerned

primarily with medical and other more scientifically documented illnesses; rather, therapists are being employed as a
new priesthood of self-fulfillment. "I have called this phenomenon," writes Frankl, "which the psychiatrist now has
to deal with so frequently, 'the existential vacuum.' What I
mean thereby is the experience of a total lack, or loss, of an
ultimate meaning to one's existence that would make life
worthwhile."[43]

A number of influential psychologists have blended
magic, mysticism, and science in the pursuit of "cures."
New Age philosophy is the guiding force behind much of
this research, as the world of the spirit is treated as though
it could be probed with the instruments with which we
observe the world outside us.

Roshi instructs us, "In Zen the aim is to produce a person
who 'drifts like clouds and flows like water.'"[44] Of course,
for cynical Westerners like myself, that sounds like nothing
more than the "weightless existence" Nietzsche predicted
would follow the "death of God." No wonder he prophesied
a "new Buddhism" would sweep the culture.

Lasch argues that "the contemporary climate is therapeutic, not religious." That is an important point, because it
means that the gospel, religious in its concerns, must
become therapeutic and promise psychological well-being.
Words like sin, grace, and redemption will have to be
replaced with sickness, support, and self-realization. This is,
in fact, just what Lasch insists has happened: "People today
hunger not for personal salvation, let alone for the restoration of an earlier golden age, but for the feeling, the
momentary illusion of personal well-being, health, and psychic security."[45] This is an aspect of what it means to live in
what Lasch has called the culture of narcissism.

A cursory scanning of Christian books and articles would
suggest that this shift from salvation to psychic well-being
has indeed taken place. Books offering techniques for self-
improvement, as we have noted before, far outnumber
books explaining God, humanity, the world, or salvation.
Christians have become almost idolatrous in their obsession

with self and an irresponsible leadership has fed the obsession instead of confronting it.

But again, this therapeutic bent is part of an older past. Harvey Cox draws a parallel between New Age "revivalists" and those of the earlier frontier:

> Salvation comes, as it did for the early Methodists, in small intense and avidly honest groups, usually gathered in sylvan retreats. But salvation, also as with the early Methodists, is never fully assured merely by a conversion. One can easily backslide (into phoniness or uptightness) and one must constantly strive to "go on to perfection." This usually required periodic perk-up visits to sensitivity groups, encounter sessions or human potential centers. There are circuit-preachers, too, the traveling revivalists and wandering specialists in psychodynamics, primal scream, basic encounter, "rolphing," . . . and techniques for inducing joy, openness, enhanced feeling and inner peace. They travel by jet instead of on horseback today.[46]

Already, however, many psychologists, among them Karl Menninger and Paul Johnson, have warned Christians not to abandon their theological vocabulary, but to explain it to a new generation. The doctrines of sin, grace, atonement, repentance, and so on, according to Menninger, are of infinite value in resolving the problems psychology attempts to answer. By mimicking psychology, Christian churches and ministries are failing to provide the sense of meaning and fulfillment they suppose psychology offers.

I am not qualified to critique psychology or therapy in general, but I am equipped to warn evangelicals that if we do not recover a theological rather than a therapeutic approach, the church will be nothing more than an apprentice to the real doctors of modern souls.

Amnesia

Another characteristic the New Age movement shares with its American past is an intense carelessness with regard to the past. Oriented to today, the movement reflects

the existential *angst* and doubt about anything more than
that. Its antipathy toward history is related to the antirational, anti-establishment, antisocial thrust. When the individual is glorified and when personal happiness becomes
the chief end of life, one no longer has to respect either the
community that has gone before him or the one in which
he presently finds himself—or indeed, for that matter, for
the one that is to come. Since each person can create his
own reality, there are no values, beliefs, or attitudes which
are shared by all—and which ought to be shared by all. The
only laws that should be imposed would be those which
keep one person from interfering with the freedom of
another individual.

As an extension of this outlook, the New Age movement
often supports a radical decentralization of the government,
laissez-faire capitalism, and eventual autocracy and anarchy.
"Having displaced religion as the organizing framework of
American culture," says Lasch, "the therapeutic outlook
threatens to displace politics as well, the last refuge of ideolo-
gy."[47] New Age leader Ferguson adds, "It promotes the
autonomous individual in a decentralized society."[48]

Hippies have become yuppies. Favoring redistribution of
wealth in the 1960s, the New Agers have wealth in the
1990s and want to keep it. "Like many ex-radicals," the hip-
pie-yuppie "has succeeded only in exchanging current therapeutic slogans for the political slogans he used to mouth
with equal disregard of their content."[49] Techniques which
cater to narcissistic self-interest demand an antisocial agenda.

Of course, if one's own inner world is the object of knowledge, there is no need for a rational, intellectual culture.
After cautioning the student against reading too many
books, Roshi refers to Nietzsche's loss of eyesight: "When
his eyesight became so poor that he could no longer read
books, he began at last to read himself."[50] The student
replies, "What sort of books are best to read when you
want to live a spiritual life?" which Roshi answers in a way
one might expect some evangelicals to respond: "A book
which has the deep ring of truth discovered through per-

sonal experience. The good book stirs the heart, fires the imagination, and leads to the resolve to let nothing stand in the way of full awakening."[51] The kind of book to avoid is the one which "clogs the mind with sticky concepts and notions"—in other words, the kind of book that tries to communicate thoughts rather than merely experiences.[52]

Secular Eschatology

We are all familiar, of course, with the influence of Darwinism in the biological sciences, but Darwinism is itself a product of Hegelian philosophy. Hegel argued that history was a process in which one radical view, then its opposite, and finally, a synthesis of the two, reigned. Each time the cycle produces a synthesis, we come closer to the truth. This, of course, leads to irrationalism, since every truth is the synthesis of a contradiction. One cannot say that "A is 'A' and 'not-A' at the same time in the same way." That is the law of noncontradiction. Yet, for Hegel, the truth was found precisely at the point one issued the contradiction.

For a recent example of this sort of thinking, one might look at Marxism. Following Hegel, Karl Marx interpreted history as reactions to the problem of economics. Marx insists that he holds no contempt for any system, since all systems are inevitable steps in the staircase leading to the utopian ideal of communism. Without something as oppressive as feudalism, there would never have been something as liberating as the peasants' uprisings. The Hegelian contradictions abound within the Marxist system itself. Marx and Lenin argued that a communist state must begin as a totalitarian dictatorship, but end in total anarchy. After reordering everything in a harsh and absolutely centralized manner, the state itself would be dissolved and dismantled.

Evolution, therefore, in Hegelian terms, is a process of thesis ("A is 'A'"), antithesis ("A is 'not-A'"), and synthesis ("A is 'A' and 'not-A' in the same way, at the same time"). This, of course, leads to nothing but irrationalism. (It is Hegelian thought that shapes process philosophy and theology, which we mentioned earlier.) New Agers like Ferguson

view themselves as "the advance scouts for the race," looking for the next step up the spiraling staircase to utopia.

According to Christianity, however, history is not evolu-
tionary. As Saint Paul speaks of the creation being "in
bondage to decay," so science has demonstrated, in the second law of thermodynamics, that the world is falling apart,
not being put back together. The Bible teaches clearly that
humans are not perfectible by nature, but fallen and needing redemption. Total restoration will not arrive until the
unveiling of the new heaven and the new earth, with our
resurrected bodies. It is Jesus Christ, the Perfect, who
makes all things new at the end of "this present evil age."

Conclusion

The New Age movement is one result of the direction
American religion has taken since the breakdown of
Protestant orthodoxy in New England. At last, after succes-
sive departures, many Americans are worshiping again at
the First Church of Eden, hanging on Lucifer's promise,
"You shall be as God, knowing both good and evil."

But where were the churches during the 1960s? What
were we doing—and what did we represent in the face of
racism, the Vietnam War, and the exploitation of Third
World countries? Later, in the 1970s, where were we during Watergate? With whom were we standing then? It
seems that when the world needed to hear another voice,
the voice of a prophet, all it heard was the baptism of the
establishment. The church was so much a part of the problem that whenever a minister mounted the pulpit, he was
expected to merely recite the creed of either the liberal or
the conservative establishment. There was something lacking of a transcendent quality.

During his ministry, Jesus was admired "because he
taught as one who had authority, and not as their teachers
of the law" (Matt. 7:29). Jesus always had something radical to say—not radical in the political sense, but in the ultimate sense. He never preached a political agenda, and yet

his transcendent, theologically-focused message had incredible political ramifications. People knew that they might not like what Jesus had to say, but they could always expect him to say something profoundly different from what they were used to hearing.

Many of the New Age leaders, according to a friend who is in contact with them, are ex-fundamentalists. They tired of being told what to believe without questioning or being able to think. They wearied of rules and expectations calculated to keep them from the world. Sick of judgment, accusation, and dogmatism, many saw the New Age movement as a cure.

· We have to have some sympathy for those who have encountered the frustration of not having questions answered, but being told, "Just believe." I am familiar with the ridiculous rules we grew up with, uncovering an intrinsic Gnostic antiworldliness within evangelicalism. But why run headlong into a full-fledged Gnostic system because of a distortion?

According to a recent poll, the highest percentage of New Agers have a Protestant background.[53] Gallup found that "superficial Christianity was alarming to many people" he surveyed.[54] The respondents were disillusioned with a "shallow and superficial" church life that could not even "deal with the basics of the faith."[55] If we cannot provide reasonable answers and a meaningful way of looking at the world, why shouldn't we expect the next generation to abandon Christianity or the possibility of finding rational answers to life's deepest questions? Said a Catholic mystic, Anthony Padovano, at a 1976 conference on meditation, "Faith is not dying in the West. It is merely moving inside."[56] But for Christians, a faith that moves inside is already dead.

Nevertheless, the New Age movement opens up new possibilities for the church. Adherents of the movement have given up on the promise science held out of solving all human problems, and they are concerned about paying attention to the spiritual side of life. This at least provides an environment in which discussions about eternity can once again take place.

In one sense, the New Age movement represents the collapse of even a superficial Protestant consensus and an environment in which Christianity is one religion among many. It presents a challenge to the evangelical churches in terms of whether we will either accommodate our message to the pseudo-needs of an increasingly pagan society, with its superstitions and magic, or whether we will sound that peculiar note which only scriptural Christianity can produce.

Ferguson throws down the gauntlet: "Now the heretics are gaining ground, doctrine is losing its authority, and [gnostic] knowing is superseding belief."[57] Before we look for solutions to the New Age movement, we ought to take its influences in evangelicalism seriously . . . before another, more hardened generation leaves our churches for the other gods.

To Each His Own 7

Thereafter we became less theological, but I am sure
more truly religious.
—Andrew Carnegie

According to many evangelical leaders, relativism is a
component of secular humanism, but one of the purposes
of this chapter is to demonstrate that a good deal of the
blame for cultural relativism must be borne by evangelicals
themselves.

D. L. Moody used to boast that he was no theologian.
According to Martin E. Marty, "When a liberal contended
that two authors wrote the book of Isaiah, Moody, asked
about his stand, shrugged off the question. . . . 'See here, it
doesn't make much difference who wrote the book any-
how.' . . . "[1] "My theology!" he exclaimed on another occasion. "I didn't know I had any. I wish you would tell me
what my theology is."[2] And yet, when asked why he com-
posed the "Reformation Symphony," the celebrated master
Felix Mendolssohn replied, "In those days, men had convictions; we moderns have opinions."

Francis A. Schaeffer noted, "T. H. Huxley spoke as a prophet in 1890 when he said there would come a day when faith would be separated from all fact, and faith would go on triumphant forever." After all, this is what Immanuel Kant proposed and Søren Kierkegaard acted out—the famous leap of faith. "This is where," Schaeffer cautioned, "not only the liberal theologians are, but also the evangelical, orthodox theologians who begin to tone down on the truth, the propositional truth of Scripture, which God has given us."[3]

Schaeffer went on to relate the response we can expect:

> Students from the London School of Economics, Harvard, and the Sorbonne, from Africa and Asia and from the ends of the earth, have come to L'Abri with their packs on their backs. But if you think they would listen to us if we were not willing to say that what Christianity teaches (what God has spoken) stands as an antithesis to its opposite, you do not understand your own children or your own age. Our credibility is already minus 5 if we do not say what is false and wrong in contrast to what is true and right. . . . Some Christians think they will be listened to more if they give in a bit at some points concerning the Scripture, but they are mistaken—they have given away the answers which are needed.[4]

And it is never maliciousness that creates theological relativism, but, most often, a mere unwillingness to spend the time and energy checking out the facts.

It has been noted throughout this volume that along with the declaration of independence from the God of Reformation orthodoxy came an emancipation from theology altogether. It seems that our forebears were attracted to the Enlightenment offer of freedom from the confining, dogmatic restraints of Old World religion and were thus drawn to the unrestrained individualism of rationalism and, later, emotionalism.

Donald G. Bloesch notes, "What is conspicuous in American church life in particular is the dissipation of doctrinal and apostolic substance. There is a preoccupation with the cultivation of the inner life and holistic salvation, but faithfulness to the apostolic faith, rediscovered and attested anew in the Reformation, is dismally lacking." He observes, "Voltaire's latitudinarian spirit has triumphed over the dogmatic stance of Calvin and Luther. Other views, we are told, should be respected because all views are fundamentally the same, though they differ superficially." Because of this accommodation, Bloesch concludes, the American church has "lost the capacity to be prophetic."[5]

As early as 1782, St. John de Crevecoeur was amazed by the multiplicity of competing sects. "Religious indifference," he said, "is imperceptibly disseminated from one end of the continent to the other; which is at the present one of the strongest characteristics of the Americans." Further, Crevecoeur reported, "Where this will reach no one can tell, perhaps it may leave a vacuum fit to receive other systems. Persecution, religious pride, the love of contradiction, are the food of what the world commonly calls religion."[6]

In his Pulitzer Prize-winning *Anti-Intellectualism in American Life*, Richard Hofstadter notes that "the combined forces of localism and revivalism greatly strengthened the hand of the heretic or the schismatic: so long as he could produce results. So long as he could produce results, who could control him?"[7] Since religion was "of the people, for the people, and by the people," the test of a creed was not its truth, but its success. In the preceding chapters we have studied some of the fundamental trends most responsible for this relativistic way of thinking. In many ways, as we shall see, evangelicalism not only has become a tragic victim of worldly relativism, but also has, to some degree, nurtured it.

First, there is the general collapse of the scientific world view, which made promises it couldn't keep. Sir John Eccles, a Nobel Prize–winning pioneer in brain research, observes that science, in trying to answer questions beyond its competence, becomes reduced to superstition. "Science," he says, "cannot explain the existence of each of us as a unique self, nor can it answer such fundamental questions as: Who am I? Why am I here? How did I come to be at a

certain place and time? What happens after death? These
are all mysteries beyond science."[8] With the Enlightenment,
science displaced Christianity as the intellectual authority,
but when science failed to provide ultimate answers itself,
relativism replaced science.

Since the existentialist thrives on despair and turns inward in self-reflection, he had plenty of reason to turn to
such maxims as the Beatles' "All We Need Is Love." In reaction to the plastic society created by the industrial, scientific, and technological revolutions, the new Romanticists
and Transcendentalists sought answers outside of a rational
framework. The Beatles' hit, "Nowhere Man," could be
viewed as a virtual hymn of existentialism. The "Nowhere
Man" sits in his "nowhere land, making all his nowhere
plans for nobody." He "doesn't have a point of view, knows
not where he's going to," and the song asks, "Isn't he a bit
like you and me?" Notice the apathy and relativism:
"doesn't have a point of view." Ironically, the culture does
not respect those who do not have a point of view while it
champions relativism! In such songs the rivers of existentialism, nihilism, and Transcendentalism merge, and we
catch a glimpse of the desperation of our culture. G. K.
Chesterton once said that when we cast aside our belief in
God, it wouldn't be that we would then believe in nothing,
but that we would believe in anything and everything.

Through the successive forces of cultural change, the
church has so diluted its message that we are poor critics of
relativism. We have come to a place in evangelical circles
where the same relativistic responses can be heard in the
narthex as one might expect to hear at the mall. Take, for
instance, the subtle but effective retort, "Christianity is a
person, not a proposition." Or, "No creed but Christ." In
1990, I was interviewed on scores of television and radio
stations across America about *The Agony of Deceit,* which I
edited. It was an anthology by evangelical leaders alerting
the Christian community to the heresies of foremost televangelists. The most frequent response I heard in those
interviews from callers and evangelical talk-show hosts

was, "How can you read these people's hearts?" "Don't they love Jesus?" "Aren't you just imposing your theology on them?" These are the responses one would expect from unbelievers, but not from brothers and sisters.

In contemporary society, if one has a conviction shaped by intense struggles and rigorous investigation, one that is not shared by a consensus of Americans, that conviction is called dogmatism. Of course, there is an unhealthy form of dogmatism—the "just believe" syndrome. Some of our relativism, therefore, can be understood as a reaction against pedantic and closed-minded fundamentalism. Our adoption of cultural relativism, however, has assisted in making it a virtual sin to be certain.

Relativism in Education

Professor Allan Bloom, in *The Closing of the American Mind*, critiques cultural relativism from a secular perspective. As he sees it, it is relativism that is closed-minded. What is more closed-minded than saying, "I will never say, 'This is true!,' and 'This is false!'"? If one cannot say, "This is true," of what use is the university? We cannot simply teach opinions; we must teach what we believe to be true—about history, about science, and so on. Established by the Puritans, Harvard still, ironically, bears this inscription on its seal: *Veritas* (Truth).

Times have changed, according to Bloom and other educators such as Mortimer J. Adler. "The purpose of education" nowadays, says Bloom, "is not to make scholars, but to provide them with a moral virtue: openness." "There is one thing a professor can be absolutely certain of," according to Bloom: "almost every student entering the university believes, or says he believes, that truth is relative." Students "have causes without content. Reason has been replaced by mindless commitment, consciousness-raising and trashy sentimentality."[9] Can we not say the same of contemporary evangelical subculture?

The Carnegie Commission report on education insists that

"in a pluralistic society" like ours, "adherence exclusively to the doctrines of any one school . . . would cause higher education to be in great dissonance with society."[10]But when did education take its cue from the masses? Wasn't it, rather, the other way around? The result is that a university student is no longer educated, with a coherent world view, but informed, with a catalogue of disconnected facts, tangled and contradictory. Bloom says a characteristic requirement of the modern student is, "I want to know what is good for me, what will make me happy." And today's students (Christian or not) are impatient with knowledge that does not promise success, offer new techniques for getting things done, or help one advance in his or her career. One would hope that at Christian colleges, at least, the humanities would be protected, but even they have caved in to the pressures of pragmatism.

Consequently, as Lasch conceives it, "Standards are deteriorating even at Harvard, Yale, and Princeton. . . . A faculty committee at Harvard reports, 'The Harvard faculty does not care about teaching.' According to a study of general education at Columbia, teachers have lost 'their common sense of what kind of ignorance is acceptable.'"[11]

In June 1988, the findings of a survey demonstrated that 75 percent of American adults cannot locate the Persian Gulf on a map and 45 percent cannot locate Central America. Respondents (these are adults, mind you) also placed New York State in thirty-seven places, from New Jersey to California. "On a world map," according to USA TODAY, "the USA can be found in India, the Soviet Union, China, and Botswana." In another survey, most American adults could not find Massachusetts, New Jersey, Missouri, Japan, Vietnam, or South Africa on a map.[12]

Educator Benjamin Stein warns, "The kids . . . are not mentally prepared to continue the society because they basically do not understand the society well enough to value it."[13] In his best-seller, Cultural Literacy, E. D. Hirsch, Jr., refers to current public education as "cafeteria-style education."[14]

There is no longer a generally accepted core of knowledge or belief. In skimming current catalogues for evangelical seminaries and colleges, one discovers a striking similarity to "cafeteria-style education." If evangelicals cannot come up with a common core of convictions, and defend them, how can we criticize the world for the same? Remember Marty's remark about evangelicals who "pick and choose truths as if on a cafeteria line."[15]

The great tradition in American education was undergirded by a great tradition in American religion. Our best and brightest centers were those established by those adhering to the Reformation faith: Harvard, Yale, Princeton, Brown, Dartmouth, Rutgers. But the great tradition in American education is undermined by the same relativism which has plagued the evangelical movement since the Second Awakening. By contemporary standards, the Puritans would be considered dogmatic. Nevertheless, according to Hofstadter, "It is doubtful that any community ever had more faith in the value of learning and intellect than Massachusetts Bay. The Puritans founded that intellectual and scholarly tradition which for three centuries enabled New England to lead the country in educational and scholarly achievement."[16]

The importance of having a well-defined theological system in the shaping of scholars is evident not only in the universities founded by Protestants, but in such institutions as Notre Dame or Loyola. While evangelical Protestants would take issue with Roman Catholic dogma (and vice versa), the importance of speaking from a larger tradition that has developed and reflected for centuries is undeniable.

Intellectual rigor demands the possibility and, indeed, the anticipation, of arriving at conclusions—and, more than that, conclusions that can be called true. But proponents of the New Age movement insist that education must continue to deny objective conclusions, claiming, in their own words, that education must demonstrate "how the learner came to be unfree . . . , about our culture's great learning disability, an educational system that emphasizes being 'right' at the expense of being open."[17] But it is just this sort of relativism and anti-intellectualism that is responsible for "our culture's great learning disability." "On the portal of the university," writes Bloom, "is written in many ways, and in many tongues, 'There is no truth—at least here."[18] In a culture of narcissism, "truth has given way to credibility, facts to statements that sound authoritative without conveying any authoritative information."[19]

And before we evangelicals offer a sanctimonious sigh about secular humanists and public education, it should be kept in mind that we do precisely the same thing when we dismiss a debate or a point of clarification on the grounds, "Well, we just can't know these things 'til we see Jesus," or, "But that's theology." We also do the same thing in our churches when clichés pass for content, pep talks for sermons, and vague sentiment for serious teaching. When we turn to the Bible, not to learn from it or to be challenged by it, but to be merely inspired, we become the very relativists we disdain. Every time someone says, "This is what this verse means to me," or "God told me . . . ," " or "I know this might not be what this verse is saying, but the application is edifying," relativism sets in.

The crisis of certainty must be countered on a number of fronts. For us especially as evangelicals, who believe God has spoken in history (not simply "to my heart"), the following are pressure points.

The Clarity of Scripture

Concerning the perspicuity of Scripture, the Reformers of the sixteenth century lamented that the church had shrouded the Bible in ambiguity. Martin Luther and John Calvin, paraphrased, put it in these words: "The Bible itself isn't ambiguous about these subjects we're addressing—the church is!" Reluctant to be vulnerable to the dangerous teachings of Scripture, the church refused to take theological stands—until the Reformation left it with no option. In fact, on the eve of the Reformation, there were twelve theological schools of thought competing for control at the University of Paris.

Calvin said, "Seldom did a minister mount the pulpit to teach. . . . Nay, what one sermon was there from which old wives might not carry off more whimsies than they could devise at their own fireside in a month?" He continued: "The first half [of the sermon] was devoted to those misty questions of the schools which might astonish the ignorant populace, while the second contained sweet stories, or humorous illustrations, by which the hearers were kept awake. Only a few expressions were thrown in from the Word of God from time to time, so they could legitimize these frivolities."[20]

I am inclined to think that most modern readers could find much in contemporary preaching that resembles Calvin's description. When the Scriptures are ignored, or not taken seriously for their doctrinal content, the people lose confidence in the ability of Scripture to speak plainly to plain people.

Luther, too, was frustrated to the point of wrath with the brilliant humanist Desiderius Erasmus, because the Dutch scholar attacked the sovereignty of God in election and the bondage of the human will—not on the basis of Scripture, but on the basis that Scripture is not clear on these things. Erasmus further reasoned, "What difference does it make?" In his response, Luther appears to be more outraged by Erasmus's relativism in matters so dear than by his theological position.

The Reformers had a name for those relativists and obscurantists who shrouded the Bible in mystery: the sophists. The original Sophists were a sect of ancient Greek philosophers led by Protagoras (490 B.C.), who believed that there is no universal truth. The slogan "Man is the measure of all things" was put forth by Protagoras, who held that the only way a person could choose between one opinion and another was on the basis of pragmatism. Is there anything new under the sun?

The Authority of Scripture

Yesteryear's liberals (e.g., Schleiermacher, Herrmann, Harnack, and Bultmann) were reared in pietism, as we learned in previous chapters. They were comfortable with a sort of Christian faith we would call evangelical in America. Distrustful of historical theology and confessional subscription, they were the first to criticize the orthodox and were interested in "the inner life . . . the inmost experiences of the Christian life."[21] "This happens," declared liberal pioneer Johann Herrmann, "only when God lifts me into communion with Himself."[22] Furthermore, he said, "This can arise in spite of wrong teaching."[23] To be sure, communion with Christ does arise in spite of a person having an incomplete or even an erroneous view on a nonessential point. Aware of my own feeble understanding, I certainly hope as much. Nevertheless, the liberals, drawing on their pietist heritage, used that statement to mean, "It doesn't matter what you know about God; just that you know him." Thus, as long as people had experiences, theology was of little consequence.

Liberalism was produced not by thought, but by feeling. The architects of theological modernism were pietists, not secularists, who wanted "heart knowledge," not "head knowledge." Consequently, they were inclined to regard doctrinal orthodoxy as unimportant. Bultmann, for instance, demythologized the miracles, the resurrection, and other supposed fables of Scripture. Today, we respond that this relativizes the faith. But Bultmann did not see it as such. "To believe in the cross of Jesus," he said, "does not mean to concern ourselves with a mythical process wrought outside us and our world, but rather to make the cross of Christ our own, to undergo crucifixion with Him."[24] Note the disdain for the objective, historical character of Christianity, for that which is "wrought outside us." Subjectivism, which so marked pietism, eventually created liberalism and continues to characterize American religion, including traditional evangelicalism.

The World Council of Churches operated, according to its

declaration in Nairobi, on the conviction that "doctrine divides, service unites." This kind of talk should sound familiar to us, although it might be more appropriate to supply "experience" for "service." Evangelicals share with liberals a fear that doctrine is divisive and, therefore, unhealthy. And yet, ironically, when I met with the administrative head of the World Council some years ago, I was told that after so many years of attempting united service without doctrinal focus, the council realized that service divided and doctrine united.

The majority of evangelical college and seminary students —more than half, according to James Davison Hunter— believe that "the Bible is the inspired Word of God, not mistaken in its teachings, but is not always to be taken literally in its statements concerning matters of science, historical reporting, etc."[25] Furthermore, "One cannot speak of ultimate truth *per se*, only ultimate truth for each believer." In other words, most of the students at evangelical institutions have already accepted the relativism of their culture, and with that, the liberal and neo-orthodox concession that faith in Christ is a spiritual matter, not dependent on external, objective facts of history. Liberalism is an educated, "no creed but Christ" religion. Though it is subjective and romantic, it at least has the courage of its convictions. The new "evangelical" variety speaks "orthotalksy"—a litany of the right words, but emptied of the usual meaning.

When truth has been defined in such terms as, "The Lord spoke to my heart . . . ," and "The Lord revealed to me . . . ," the objective authority of Scripture loses its importance. But we must contend for the fact that, just as God has acted and saved outside of us, in history, so he has spoken outside of us, in history. From those who say, "God told me . . . ," I want the details. What was his voice like? "Like the voice of rushing waters" (Rev. 1:15)? What was his face like? Even Moses couldn't see God's face, but evangelists based in Tulsa can. And how did you feel when God spoke to you? Like Isaiah, who after seeing a vision of God, not even face to face, said, "Woe unto me. I am a man of unclean lips"?

Nine times out of ten, the person will respond, "Well, the words, of course, weren't audible. But you do believe that God still speaks to us, don't you?" they ask. Of course I do. He has said more than I will ever in this lifetime be able to comprehend. But that voice is confined to holy Scripture.

The Knowledge of Scripture

Bloom put it this way: "As the respect for the Sacred—the latest fad—has soared, real religion and knowledge of the Bible have diminished to the vanishing point."[26] George Lindbeck, at Yale University, makes a similar comment:

> The leaders of the Enlightenment . . . were not believers, but they were biblically literate and biblically cultured. Conversely, Bible-believing fundamentalists sometimes know remarkably little of the content of scripture. . . . When I first arrived at Yale, even those who came from nonreligious backgrounds knew the Bible better than most of those now who come from churchgoing families. . . . Playing fast and loose with the Bible needed a liberal audience in the days of Norman Vincent Peale, but now, as the case of Robert Schuller indicates, professed conservatives eat it up. . . . The culture of Christians as well as of non-Christians has been de-Christianized, and the language of public discourse has become dangerously feeble.[27]

One reason the Bible fails to be clear and authoritative is that so many Christians do not have a grasp of its major themes. It's a lack of knowledge, of teaching and expository preaching. Children can grow up in some evangelical churches and, with the exception of a few proof texts and "promises," be biblically and doctrinally illiterate. In fact, some time ago, I spoke at a Christian high school on the subject of the Protestant Reformation. It was an interdenominational, fundamentalist-type school. At the beginning, I asked for a show of hands indicating how many could define "justification." When no hands appeared, I said, "I won't ask for a definition. How many have ever heard of 'justification'?" Out of seventy Christian high school students, only one girl raised her hand, affirming that she had indeed heard of that doctrine by which, Luther said, the church stands or falls.

A Gallup poll in 1984 found that "more evangelicals believe in biblical inerrancy than actually read the Bible regularly or possess even rudimentary Bible knowledge (e.g., 50% of the evangelicals could not name even five of the Ten Commandments)."[28]

And yet, many evangelicals are having daily "quiet times" in which the Bible is being read. Nevertheless, if your quiet times were like mine, one might pick a "promise" verse out of a box or read a devotional that begins with a Bible verse and then goes on to tell a story about the author's experience; but serious study of God's Word is dismally lacking. Until we stop thinking of our faith in merely subjective, experiential terms, the Bible will be nothing more than a source of quotes for wall plaques and greeting cards.

"Is Your Interpretation Correct?"

I wish I had a dime for every time I have heard someone say, "Well, that's your interpretation!" The phrase is sometimes followed by, "There are good Christian men on both sides." Of course, nobody is questioning the moral character or the personality traits of those who hold other views, but the truth or error of the positions.

We have to be careful in using this reaction the same way secular relativists use it. Obviously, if I am arguing a position or exegeting a text, what comes out is "my opinion." But can't "my opinion" be correct or false? Our teachers in school gave us their interpretation of history, science, math, English, and art. But does that invalidate the facts they taught us? Of course not. It is impossible to tell a story or explain a theory without interpretation. Does the existence of two opposing interpretations mean there cannot be a true one? Two historians can argue over whether World War II could have been averted had the Allies stopped Hitler before he had taken Austria. And the two historians may both be wrong, but can they both be right at the point where their views contradict?

The question, then, is not, "Is it your interpretation?" but "Is your interpretation correct?" This brings up the issue of comparative religion. At one time, scholarship generally contrasted biblical faith with alternatives. Now scholarship compares them. This is just one more result of secularization (hence, relativism). Harvey Cox explains:

> Sometimes one gets the impression that religious pluralism is the only thing worth talking about. . . . Instead of emphasizing the uniqueness of the ancient Hebrew faith, Old Testament scholars search for parallels with the Canaanites. New Testament students compare the Pauline epistles and the synoptic gospels with Gnostic scrolls and Buddhist or Hindu texts. . . . They cannot avoid the question of truth forever. Economists who investigate rival theories of savings and inflation must decide how to invest their own money. Students of comparative religion eventually have to decide how they are going to live their lives and make their decisions.[29]

For so long, many evangelicals have been told to blindly ignore options; now they are actually encouraged in some quarters to blindly embrace them. While the culture commands us to postpone conclusions indefinitely (as William James told us, "We don't know which one will work best in the long run"), the Christian must speak with conviction where God has spoken.

"Let's Just Love Jesus"

Evangelicals must be congratulated for their devotion and zeal. If only we could combine zeal and theology in warm, dedicated hearts and minds! Evangelicals have a tendency to refer to Christ these days in very personal terms as a friend, and he is indeed the friend who sticks closer to us than a brother. Sometimes he is also spoken of as a lover, which is much like the way medieval mystics thought of him. Romanticism transformed theology into sentimentalism, and we can see this shift in our hymnody. The older hymns combined passion and profound doctrinal themes. Nothing stirs the heart like "A Mighty Fortress," and yet it says so much about God and his trustworthiness. Other divine attributes are celebrated in "How Great Thou Art," as the writer uses the natural, objective world as a springboard for reflection on God's greatness; it's hard to keep the tears back with "O Sacred Head, Now Wounded," and "Crown Him with Many Crowns" transports me to the heavenlies where I get a foretaste of seeing my King in all his regal glory.

In other words, the shift from the older to the Victorian Romantic hymns is, generally speaking, a change in emphasis from a God-centered, objective, historical faith that is for me, but outside of me, to a man-centered, subjective, existential faith that is almost exclusively concerned with personal experiences with the Spirit or with Jesus.

This shift is reflected in the comment, "Let's just love Jesus—theology just gets in the way." First, it must be confessed that we can and have obscured the simplicity of loving Christ with silly distinctions. Nevertheless, theology is nothing more than the study of God. If learning more about God gets in the way of loving him, what hope do we have of discovering the very attributes which inspire our devotion, reverence, and worship? If indeed theology gets in the way of "just loving Jesus," we have apologies to make to the Mormons and Jehovah's Witnesses, and to many others besides. I have Mormon friends who insist that they love Jesus. They are moral, upstanding people who go to church two or three times more often than we. And yet, most evangelicals insist that Mormons are not Christians—but why? Because of theological, doctrinal differences!

Sometimes, it is true, we can become so caught up in being correct about our view of Christ that we, oddly enough, have no time or energy left for simply communing with him. Furthermore, sometimes we become so preoccupied with learning about God that we grow cold and insensitive to God himself in the meantime. Hence, we erroneously attack sensitivity for sentimentalism; piety for pietism; mystery for mysticism.

Nevertheless, we never speak of having a personal relationship with other people apart from knowing certain things about them. It would be silly to think we could have a deep relationship with someone about whom we knew very little. And it is the same with God. It is possible to have a deep knowledge without a deep relationship, but impossible to have a deep relationship without a corresponding depth in understanding. The fascination of both heart and mind is required as we "grow in the grace *and* knowledge of our Lord and Savior Jesus Christ" (2 Pet. 3:18, italics added).

Therefore, I would argue that evangelicals have not thought through sufficiently what it means to "just love Jesus." How are we to fulfill this, the greatest commandment? Said Jesus, "Love the Lord your God with all your *heart*, and with all your *soul* and with all your *mind*'" (Matt. 22:37, italics added). He does not prescribe either emotion-centered or intellect-centered love, but wants our total being involved in the process of loving God. Furthermore, we are commanded to be transformed "by the renewing of your mind" (Rom. 12:2). It is the mind which interprets a verse or a comment; it is the intellect which reflects on a relationship. Before we ever feel or experience something, it is a thought. It is our reflection on someone or something that makes us angry, excited, reluctant or gracious. Before we can begin experiencing new feelings or making new decisions, we must undergo a "renewing [of] the mind."

At this point, too, we ought to define orthodoxy in relationship to the question of theology. I hardly ever hear evangelicals use the term *orthodox* in a purely positive, unreserved sense. Often, it is a pejorative. But the word means "correct praise." Correct praise, or worship, is the goal of correct theology. Doctrine is never an end in itself, but a warden for our conscience, emotions, and will, guiding us in correctly worshiping God. Jesus said, "He who worships must worship in Spirit and in truth." Worship involves the total person—the mind to grasp the biblical truth, the senses (for instance, with holy communion) to taste, see, and smell the truth, the heart to sense the meaning of that truth grasped, the will to act upon that truth, and the affections to sustain that action. Further, the body itself must be employed in worship and service. With this wholistic view, worship can be easily incorporated into one's lifestyle.

Suddenly, a fishing trip to the lake becomes an opportunity to try out a bit of worship. The senses—the smell of the pine-laced fresh air, the lush forest and towering mountains, with nothing but the sound of birds chirping echoing across the lake. The intellect takes over and reflects on the information the senses have gathered. Analyzing the data, the mind notes the relation of this information to a passage in the Psalms or to a childhood experience and all of this reminds one of a particular attribute or action of God. As a result of this reflection, a chill runs down the person's spine—the scene is emotionally powerful. When we begin to worship like this in everyday life, it will be reflected in our work at the office, at home, at school, wherever we are. The more we gain a sense of God's being there in our everyday existence, the more devout we actually become.

Thus, we can no more single out one of these activities (thinking, sensing, feeling, choosing, or acting) and call it "loving Jesus" or "orthodoxy" than we can single out the mouth, the esophagus, or the stomach and call it digestion!

Dogmatism Breeds Closed-Mindedness

There has been a good deal of narrow-minded, anti-intellectual dogmatism: "God said it, I believe it, and that settles it"—that type of thinking which avoids reflection, argumentation, and the challenging of our interpretations of what it is in fact that God has said.

There is a good deal of this in our circles, where people will sometimes say, "Well, we're not going to change each other's minds anyway." If there is no possibility of changing our minds, what is the point in expecting others, especially non-Christians, to change their minds by embracing the gospel? If Christianity can be proved true, it must also be at least theoretically possible for it to be proved false. We must take that chance when we challenge our convictions. But we are afraid of that risk, so we sometimes close our minds.

Doctrine ought not to be embraced simply because it is that with which we were reared. This, called "implicit faith," was the "faith" against which the Reformers railed. Thus, evangelicals are not supposed to embrace anything simply on the basis that it is what they were told to believe, but they must test their beliefs. This is what it means to be, in their words, "Reformed and always reforming according to the Word of God."

Surely this kind of thinking does not breed closed-mindedness, but evangelicalism has, in many ways, stopped thinking. When that happens, there is either defection (due to boredom) or closed-minded, dead orthodoxy. Doctrine, however, can be the very stimulus we need to wake up our minds. I know it was that way for me. It was feelings or the expectation of feelings that bored me. When I was beginning to think that Christianity had little use for the life of the mind, Saint Paul invited me to climb the Alps of Romans, from which the open vistas appeared boundless. Suddenly, the Bible became a book of transforming thoughts and truths. Our analytical skills are atrophied for lack of exercise. And we need desperately to recover the intellectual vitality which Christianity has inspired in the best of times.

Jacques Ellul, the French law professor and Christian commentator, pointed out that "propaganda uses facts not to support an argument but to exert emotional pressure" (Lasch, p. 144). There is too much propaganda and too little genuine reflection in society generally and in the church specifically. We have a chance to change this tendency and to lead our contemporaries, as our forebears once did in the ultimate search.

How can we explode the myth of our secular contemporaries that there are no absolutes while we downplay the possibility or, indeed, the necessity of arriving at orthodox conclusions ourselves? The illusion normally adopted by our neighbors is that the more liberal one's convictions, the more open-minded the individual must be. We accept this illusion when we label anything that is different from our position "liberal." In some circles, if someone is not willing to say that all Roman Catholics go to hell, he is a "liberal." If another wants to read widely in both Christian and blatantly non-Christian literature, he, too, is suspected of having "liberal" tendencies.

But being liberal is not the same as being open-minded. In fact, that is the point Bloom, Adler, and others are making in their criticism of modern education. Christians have a Bible which invites them to "test the spirits." "Come," God invites, "let us reason together." The early Christians even tested the apostles by the standard of Scripture "to prove whether what they were teaching was true." In other words, these people did not take everything they were told on blind faith. Theirs was a reasonable faith.

Subtly, evangelicalism has accepted the myth that historic Christianity has lost the intellectual battle and that modernism has shattered the ancient biblical writings. So we give up on reason and resort to propaganda. But the truth is that the direction of archaeology, biology, and even biblical studies has shifted a good deal since the 1920s and 1930s. Just as evangelicals are gradually losing confidence in the objective, historic, factual trustworthiness of Christianity, many non-Christian scientists, historians, and other fact-finders are becoming increasingly impressed with the weight of the evidence. A Princeton philosopher, Diogenes Allen, encourages,"There is therefore no need for Christians to continue to be defensive. . . . The philosophical and scientific bases for excluding the possibility of God have collapsed. . . . The conviction that we live in a self-contained universe can no longer be supported by a philosophic consensus."[30]

Don't retreat! That is the good news in all of this. Now is the time not for a wild advance to the front, but for training, so we become better prepared to present the case in coming years.

"We Need Balance!"

For so long Americans have been a reactionary lot. And that has not left Christians unaffected. Polarizations abound between Christians on the right and left; between those who hold to literalistic creation science and theistic evolutionists; believers who carelessly flaunt their liberties and those who insist on restricting them. The cry "Balance!" comes at a time when we feel torn.

At the same time, as Calvin cautioned, "Nothing is more unbalanced than absolute balance." For many, "balance" is another word for compromise, and there are times when compromise is necessary. But most often, compromise is an easy way out of confrontation; it circumvents our analytical processes. We don't have to give an issue the intellectual energy it otherwise commands. Instead of thinking through an issue, we simply take a middle position between what we perceive as extremes. In many cases, such a "balanced" person is at a loss for words when one asks the person to explain his or her view.

Earlier, I pointed out the influence of Hegel's rather pragmatic approach to truth. One makes a statement on one side; that statement is contradicted by someone else, and, finally, the two contradictory positions are blended. This is called dialectic, and it still permeates our thinking, although it has probably been characteristic of Americans long before Hegel. You will recall Crevecoeur's surprise at the American's "love of contradiction" at the end of the eighteenth century.

Contradictions are never tolerated in day-to-day living. When we hear a politician say one thing one minute and the opposite the next, we say he is lying. When a police officer asks us if we knew we were exceeding the speed limit, it's a "yes" or "no" question. Nevertheless, when it comes to thinking deeply about our philosophy of life or our theological orientation, we revel in contradictions! But we call it balance.

One of my favorites, as a Reformed believer, is the designation *Calminian*, a Calvinist-Arminian hybrid. Calvinists believe that God does everything in salvation and that humans do absolutely nothing; Arminians believe that God does some things in salvation and that humans do other things. In other words, Calvinism is monergistic (one working) and Arminianism is synergistic (two working together). One is either a monergist or a synergist, but belief in one cancels out the other. A moderate Calvinist or *Calminian* is someone who has not been able to come to a clear, logical conclusion in this matter. "But it's biblical!" I hear someone saying. That, of course, raises the question as to whether the Bible adheres to the law of noncontradiction. As evangelicals we insist that the Bible does not contradict itself, and when we do this, we confess our conviction that the Bible does indeed adhere to the law of noncontradiction. Therefore, it would be impossible for a position to be biblical if it demanded contradiction.

While the truth may be "yes, in one sense," and "no, in another," it cannot be "yes and no" in the same way at the same time. Neither reaction (imbalance), synthesis, nor contradiction are sound approaches. None of these require effort or conviction, and relativism is the result. Truth doesn't come on a sliding scale and lie "somewhere in between." When people insist upon that, we ought to ask them, "Exactly where in between?" In most cases, they simply haven't the vaguest idea what that position is and how it can be defended. So we have to be careful with that plea for balance and find out what it is exactly that someone means by the appeal. We do not always have to agree, but we do have to be clear. Without clarity, human discussion and social and intellectual discourse is rendered meaningless.

The Practical Effects of Relativism

Not only does relativism muddle our heads; it confuses our hearts. It ultimately brings us to the place where we not only fail to think deeply about certain things, but to where we don't even feel deeply. We become apathetic, and that is seen throughout our culture. We are driven not so much in modern America by fear or joy, but by apathy. We just don't care about life anymore. Evidence for this can be seen in the search for an anesthetic to deaden the pain of being alive—drugs, entertainment, workaholism, alcoholism, pornography, or even suicide.

Relativism kills protest and passion. When the students of the 1960s protested, they were operating on borrowed capital. One cannot set out to cry, "Justice!" or to cry, "Reform!" if there is no objective standard to which one appeals for such notions. The leaders of the New Age movement tell us we are autonomous individuals and that the only absolutes are those which lead us on toward self-realization. For the 1960s that meant drugs and for the 1990s it means materialism. What will it mean in the next century? What will America's narcissists require for self-fulfillment and at whose expense will it be provided?

When we resist apartheid in South Africa (or in North America, for that matter), we are being dogmatic. When we insist that everyone is created in the image of God, that is a dogmatic doctrinal assertion, a theological statement of faith. That one doctrinal absolute defines the value of such causes as the pro-life struggle, the resolve to decrease homelessness, and so on. Without dogmatism, slavery would still be an American and a British institution. Slavery worked; it helped prosper the national economy. But it was wrong. Without the dogmatism of Rosa Parks, the black woman who refused to sit in the back of the bus, and the dogmatism of the marchers in Selma, Alabama, who, in 1965, dared to contradict the government's and society's status quo, in spite of being attacked by two hundred state police with tear gas, nightsticks, and whips—were it not for such dogmatism, injustices like this would persist to this day. It is not a mistake that all of these protests began in churches. Those modern relativists who insist dogmatically on justice or truth are using the borrowed capital of a Christian past.

Today's pop music, with notable exceptions, reflects an apathy with regard to the serious issues of modern life. Aside from occasional benefit recordings, the greatest portion of "Top 40" music is upbeat, shallow, and suitable for dancing, but not for powerful thoughts and emotions. And, oddly enough, it is precisely this "Top 40" style which dominates the entire Christian music industry. Often described in the visual arts as "viewer consumerism," much modern art, too, has taken on a purely emotional, noncognitive relativism. Instead of employing shapes, colors, and textures in the interest of a theme, much of modern art drops the theme altogether: Style without content; a medium without a message. This intellectual relativism does the same to literature. T. S. Eliot wrote, "You only have to examine the mass of newspaper leading articles, the mass of political exhortation, to appreciate the fact that good prose cannot be written by a people without convictions."[31]

In Christian circles, relativism is decried, but usually in purely moral terms. Nevertheless, there is no basis for moral absolutes apart from theological absolutes. For something to violate an aspect of practice, it must first have violated an article of faith. If we cannot tell each other, much less the world, what Christianity definitively teaches in clear doctrinal terms, we have no reason to expect anything but intolerance from our unbelieving neighbors when we try to enforce upon them moral absolutes.

Without the dogmatism of Luther and Calvin, the gospel would not have been revived in the sixteenth century. So many look to this oak for shade, but do not recognize the dogmatism its roots require. If we cannot say, for instance, that "the doctrine of justification means 'X' and does not mean 'Y,' and all Christians must believe this," then we cannot issue edicts in the moral arena either. Of course, there is rampant ethical relativism. Oxford Analytica remarks that "anyone who views the [Supreme] Court's future through the glass of recent history must feel a sense of some missing dimension in its performance. What is missing, especially in expanding areas of constitutional protection, is any coherent body of values."[32] Nevertheless, a coherent body of values depends on a coherent body of beliefs, and if we as evangelicals are unsure about the latter, we cannot expect to achieve the former. We cannot presume to think like relativists and act like absolutists.

Conclusion

As American religion was called upon to serve the practical interests of the people (civil religion), and now the interests of the self (therapeutic religion), it has moved from pragmatism to existentialism, and, consequently, to relativism. If there is no objective meaning, as existentialists argue, we are left only with working solutions which provide the most useful rather than the most faithful interpretations of reality. But we must share the blame. George Lindbeck observes, "Pietists were wary of any use except that of legitimating and evoking a particular kind of religious experience."[33] And that is precisely what modernism accepted as the extent of religion's role.

But the postmodern situation is very different. We have the opportunity to present a reasonable, intellectually credible Christianity to our contemporaries in a way that will sound like an entirely new religion to most of them. The scientific world view has failed to provide rational, satisfying answers to the ultimate questions of human existence. If Christians can demonstrate that Christianity answers those questions, its absolute claims will be embraced; if we cannot, they will go on believing that there are no true answers at all. If, in other words, we do not provide meaningful answers, relativism is the only alternative.

Today's evangelicals may be tomorrow's liberals (today's liberals, on the other hand, might be tomorrow's evangelicals) unless we can convince each other that propositional truth is as important as (indeed, the basis of) our experience of knowing Christ. Until we are convinced that being convinced, after careful and honest investigation, is acceptable, until we believe that knowing about God is fundamental to knowing Him personally, evangelicalism will continue to offer fewer and fewer meaningful answers and so, ironically, fewer and fewer meaningful experiences. We must not fail to revive thoughtful, convincing Christianity —for a culture that so desperately cries for a place to stand and a transcendent Word from its Creator.

The Loss
of Community 8

America is one vast, terrifying anti-community.
—Charles Reich, *The Greening of America*

Charles Reich, in his celebrated social critique of the 1970s, predicted the coming American revolution as a reaction to disorder, poverty, private power, unmanaged technology, the decline of democratic involvement in the political process, the meaninglessness of work, the loss of self, and the absence of community. It is hoped that this book has addressed some of these themes with Christian concern. It is that last problem on the list, absence of community, which must now receive our attention.

Reich captures what for many of our contemporaries is the status quo:

The great organizations to which most people give their working and the apartments and suburbs to which they return at night are equally places of loneliness and alienation. Modern living has obliterated place, locality, and neighborhood, and given us the anonymous separateness of our existence. The family, the most basic social system, has been ruthlessly stripped to its functional essentials. Friendship has been coated over with a layer of impenetrable artificiality as men strive to live roles designed for them. Protocol, competition, hostility, and fear have replaced the warmth of the circle of affection which might sustain man against a hostile universe.[1]

The roots of alienation, loneliness, and the loss of community can be discovered in much of our own evangelical history. It is a grave problem in society and no less troubling in the churches. Perhaps by gaining a better grasp on the problem, we can be better equipped to transform our introverted, isolated contemporaries with the communion of the saints.

Individualism

Seeking freedom from traditional norms in favor of self-expression, popular culture in the 1960s issued its own declaration of independence. This sent American culture into the "Me Decade" of the seventies, which has become the "Me Decade*s*."

Nevertheless, I think the problem is much more complicated than this. To be sure, the 1960s represented a turning point. Yet, rather than revolution, I am tempted to call it a renewal. The drive for autonomy, self-assertion, and independence has reasserted itself throughout our nation's history. The revivals of the last century (inaugurated with the Second Awakening) enabled a Jacksonian democracy to elect not only its rulers, but also its God and creed. Previously, Christians were organized into a holy commonwealth. "Man," said the Puritans, "is a sociable creature—he is made for society." They added, "That saying, 'Every man for himself and God for us all' is devilish."

Gradually, the idea of a covenant community gave way to a vision of collected individuals. Faith was not so much a mutual conviction regarding creedal statements and a consequent common experience, but an individual experience—more to the point, a decision which each person could understand in his own way. Theology aside, sects emerged throughout the last century. Each appealed to the individualistic impulses of the romantic age.

During this period, the poet Walt Whitman exulted:

> Divine am I inside out, and I
> make holy whatever I touch or
> am touched from . . .
>
> I dote on myself, there is that lot of
> me and all so luscious.
> Each moment and whatever happens
> thrills me with joy.
> —*Song of Myself*

The Puritan was concerned that even his calling served the neighborhood or commonwealth rather than himself. He hardly doted on himself. Even religious activities were not to be done from selfish motives. God has justified him, having punished Christ in his place. Acceptance had been freely given, not achieved. Therefore, even developing one's personal relationship with Christ at the expense of the community was viewed as antisocial and, consequently, anti-Christian behavior. One no longer had to work for his own salvation (for instance, by helping others), so he could give himself to the good of others from unselfish motives. Puritan William Gurnall insisted that the one who was truly pious "did others more good in this world than himself in the next."

One's energies were not to be spent hoping to earn God's favor. If salvation were by grace alone, religious piety and morality would have to be judged in terms of how they served God and neighbor in this life, not oneself in the next. Said a Puritan divine, Thomas Goodwin, "To be proficient in 'holy duties' is indeed more sweet to a man's own self, but to be proficient in our calling is more profitable to others—to the Church, the commonwealth, or the family—and so may glorify God more." Reading the Bible and praying on company time is selfish. One must never place his own spiritual well-being above that of the community.

Individualism has robbed many Christians of the joy of what the Apostles' Creed calls "the communion of the saints." Martin E. Marty fears that evangelicals threw off Old World creeds just to write "creeds and myths that defend rugged individualism and play down the community of the whole 'people of God.'" We referred to one Transcendentalist, the poet Walt Whitman. Another Transcendentalist turned process philosopher, Alfred North Whitehead, demonstrates the individualistic orientation of American religion in general. According to Marty, Whitehead said that "religion is what a person does with his solitariness." "In biblical religion," Marty insists, "it has to do with what he does with community. American religion made Whitehead's definition understandable and placed the biblical definition almost beyond reach."[2] Marty concludes,

> Little religious value is associated in historic Christianity with the idea of the individual off by himself or herself, competing against all others, often in the name of God. The Dean of Harvard Divinity School, Krister Stendahl, has effectively argued that American Christians have often twisted biblical concerns. Their kind of salvation-talk is egocentric. "What are you doing for *me*, God; who cares what happens to the larger community?" . . . Being rescued is more important than building the created world or serving others.[3]

With the rise of pietism came the rise of individualistic introspection, the emphasis on one's personal relationship with Jesus. Of course, as Billy Graham says, "God has no grandchildren." Nevertheless, he does not have a child, but children; not merely a saved person, but a saved people.

The entire Old Testament paints the portrait of a God working with a chosen nation, a communion of saints. When he works with or through individuals uniquely, it is presented as just that—an exception. Moses, on God's behalf, did not tell Pharaoh, "Let my person" or "persons go," but, "Let my people go" (Exod. 5:1). "I will take you as my own people, and I will be your God'" (Exod. 6:7). They are not "people" but "the people of his inheritance" (Deut. 4:20). "We are the people of his pasture," sang the psalmist (Ps. 95:7).

It is no different in the New Testament. The Old Testament promises made to the nation Israel are fulfilled in the "true Israel," the church. Statements made concerning the Jewish nation in the Old Testament are applied to New Testament believers: Saint Peter said, "You are a chosen people, a royal priesthood, a holy nation, a people belonging to God. . . . Once you were not a people, but now you are the people of God" (1 Pet. 2:9–10). Furthermore, Jesus died "for the sins of the people" (Heb. 2:17; 5:3); he "loved the church and gave himself up for her [collectively] . . . to present her to himself as a radiant church" (Eph. 5:25, 27). God has in mind a saved community, not just saved individuals.

Our churches are one of the last bastions of community, and yet, they do not escape individualism; indeed, much of evangelicalism has contributed to the modern situation. Many of us drive to church, listen to the sermon, say "hello" to our circle of friends, and return home without ever having really experienced community. Earlier evangelicalism was so focused on corporate spirituality that communion was taken with a common cup. Today, however, many churches offer recipes for personal growth without relating that growth to the larger group.

We hear endless sermons on spiritual gifts and how the body of Christ is supposed to operate in concert. And yet, our services often are made up of the professionals (particularly the choir) who entertain us and the individual, separate believers who are entertained. One example of corporate worship is the Anglican *Book of Common Prayer* (used by the Puritans and by Episcopalians). In such liturgical services, the congregation is led in worship and response. Each member is part of the choir. The whole church responds to God's attributes and works in unison, reciting Psalms and ancient anthems. The readings recall God's presence and power among his saints throughout history, and the worshiper feels a part of an ancient community. In a world of cold individualism there is a place of warm refuge with friends past and present.

To counter the individualism of church life and the consequent loss of community, many churches have resorted to a religious equivalent of encounter groups in which the truly committed find mutual accountability and concern. In some cases, Bible studies, prayer groups, and small groups even begin to take the place of public worship. "I don't get much out of the formal service," one often hears, "so I just go to the fellowship meetings." Thus, fellowship becomes an end in itself. God is dishonored, but so is the individual, since he or she misses out on the role one might have in the drama of corporate public worship.

Gallup polls indicate that 68 percent of America's unchurched adult population believes in Christ's physical resurrection. Two in five unchurched adults say they have "made a personal commitment to Jesus Christ."[4] Evidently, that "personal commitment to Jesus Christ" has nothing to do with his church. Louis Harris approvingly concludes that religious faith "is contained within the individual rather than reflected in slavish loyalty to church attendance or to the letter of the dogma of a particular religion."[5]

We call that "slavish loyalty" discipleship.

Part of the individualistic cynicism toward the community is grounded in anti-institutionalism, characteristic of Americans since the Jacksonian era. The idea was that the individual, left to himself, could achieve his dreams. Institutions stifled the spirit, it was assumed. This anti-institutionalism was perhaps no clearer than in the church world. "I have church in my own home in my own ways" it has been said.

Never has there been such a cynicism toward institutions in general and the church in particular. In 1966, a time of sexual liberation and anti-religious revolution, 42 percent of Americans held the institutional church in high esteem.

That has fallen twenty percentage points—to 20 percent in 1986! The public has more confidence in the media, the military, education, medicine, the Supreme Court, Congress, and the White House than in the institutional church.[6]

It is true that we enjoy a personal relationship with Christ, but only as we are a part of the church, which enjoys a corporate relationship with Christ as his body. Saint Cyprian wisely said, "Outside the church there is no salvation." Calvin added, "He cannot have God for his Father who does not take the church for his mother." The fellowship of the early church was so lively because the believers understood that "the Lord added to their number daily those who were being saved" (Acts 2:47). As John Stott says, "God did not add them to the church without saving them and he didn't save them without adding them to the church."

Materialism, Narcissism, Hedonism

Whitman's poem, *Song of Myself*, underscores the tendency to "dote on myself" in an individualistic consciousness. Sexual acts are detached from sexual commitment; taking is not related to giving; spending is not related to saving. The community is a collection of self-interested individuals commited to "the pursuit of happiness." Even religion can become a self-centered, individualistic, narcissistic preoccupation.

According to Robert N. Bellah and his co-authors in *Habits of the Heart,* the politics of the 1980s had as the "primary aim of government . . . to safeguard the peace and security necessary to allow self-reliant individuals to pursue their largely economic aims in freedom."[7] Thus, said Ronald Reagan, "I have never looked for a business that's going to render a service to mankind. I figure that if it employs a lot of people and makes a lot of money, it is in fact rendering a service to mankind. Greed is involved in everything we do. I find no fault with that."[8] With Gordon Gekko, the tycoon in the film *Wall Street,* we could cheer, "Greed is good!" In that same film, Bud, the young, upwardly mobile employee, ponders, "Adjust! Transactions, not relationships, count. Forget institutional culture—action. Keep on dialing for dollars!"[9]

It was Tom Wolfe who described the 1970s as the "Me Decade." Now, after chronicling the heedless materialism of the 1980s in his immensely popular novel, *The Bonfire of Vanities*, Wolfe tells us, "It is the decade of money fever. It's almost impossible for people to be free of the burning itch for money. It's a decade not likely to produce heroic figures."[10]

"In the past," says Harris, "materialism and vanity were taken as sure signs of the decline and fall of a civilization," yet the current attitude seems to be that individual well-being takes priority over the commonwealth. No more evident is this self-interest than in the tragic justification of abortion as a means of birth control on the basis of the mother's psychological well-being. Only 53 percent of Americans believe most children have loving parents, and child abuse is on the rise.

It is no wonder that an outlook which defies the self will eventually lead to the disintegration of the self. That is because one can only find his identity in context. A fish has no identity outside of water; a lifelong actor feels alienated and lonely away from the stage; a child loses his identity apart from his family. The water, the stage, the family— these are not constricting, limiting tyrannies, but cradles of individual freedom and identity.

Genuine selfhood is not found in absolute independence, but in a context of community. Absolute independence, freedom, and autonomy lead to alienation and loneliness. We often say that unattended children would rather have discipline than anarchy and autonomy. "At least the child knows someone cares," we say when a parent demands that a son or a daughter observe a curfew. And yet we deny that principle in our own lives, entertaining the notion that true freedom and self-esteem are found in individualistic, narcissistic independence.

We need to depend on people and on God. We need to

recognize our finitude. There is no security in isolation, only fear and doubt.

Pragmatism

In our church life, there is too much of a focus on programs over people. Do we, as ministers, view people in our congregations as sheep to be comforted, instructed, catechized, and led—or as incremental growth? And are they being led to view each other as human beings with needs which are beyond simple formulae, techniques, programs, or methods?

I am concerned that certain church-growth strategies have trivialized both the person and the community. Employing Madison Avenue technologies, neighborhoods become "target audiences" for church telemarketing. Those who are reached by telephone during these telemarketing crusades are asked to respond to a series of survey questions. While my own next-door neighbor might not even know my name, I will participate in a telemarketing drive, phoning strangers across town? Has it really come to that?

I was even approached once with a church-growth strategy involving recorded messages. A man or a woman answers the phone and hears a recording inviting him or her to a "warm, loving, caring church—where each person is important"!

Do we see our neighborhoods as a gathering of families and individuals who need the Lord, or as demographics? How easily one can contrast today's church-growth strategy with God's. The divine method is outlined in Acts: "They devoted themselves to the apostles' teaching and to the fellowship, to the breaking of bread, and to prayer. Everyone was filled with awe" (Acts 2:42, 43). In this setting, with this straightforward strategy, "there were added about three thousand souls" in one day (v. 41)! The only possible explanation: "The Lord added to [the church] daily those who were being saved" (v. 47).

In the apostolic church, then, simple truth—as it was taught and proclaimed, as it was experienced in holy com-

munion, in genuine fellowship, and in common prayer, and
as it was spread in evangelism and outreach—became the
attractive features of a church in the midst of an individualistic, materialistic, pagan culture. No gimmicks were
required. While the apostolic church must not be romanti-
cized, it was home to disciples who sought the truth, not to
consumers who sought a fix. Consequently, its fellowship
was real and lasting. It was a cottage rather than a supermarket and people developed closely-knit bonds—not
because of their common self-interest (happiness, excitement, success, joy, and other consumer wants), but because
of their common intimacy with Jesus of Nazareth, the
ascended Son of God.

Our suburban superchurches tend to attract crowds, sometimes with spectacular shows, programs, and oratory.
Outsmarted and outspent, the smaller neighborhood parishes
go on meeting simpler needs, such as providing community.

If we are to have community in our churches, we will
have to consider abandoning the superchurches as our
model. Such spiritual empires tend (unintentionally) to
cater to our collective narcissism. Positive preaching (con-
frontational preaching has not found a spot on most
church-growth lists I've seen), uplifting music, inspiring testimonies are for happy people, the "beautiful people" who
haven't a care in the world.

But didn't Jesus come "to seek and to save that which
was lost"? Did he not say, "It is not the righteous who need
a physician, but the sick"? Is it not our own Scriptures
which teach, "The Lord is close to those who have a broken
and crushed spirit"? And that he "opposes the proud, but
gives grace to the humble"? The church is not for self-satis-
fied masses, but for sinners who are persevering through
life's storms, with the help of brothers and sisters who care.

A final consideration of pragmatism's contribution to a
loss of community is the role of Christian media. Not long
ago, I happened to notice an advertisement for CBN's "700
Club" on that same network. A woman, desperate for consolation, was driving home and remembered the telephone

number for the "700 Club"counselors. In the commercial, she pulls over to the side of the road, holding back the tears as she dials a stranger in Virginia Beach.

Presuming this fictional woman were a believer, why didn't she call a friend from church? Why do televangelists speak to me as if they know me personally, as if I were sending money to a relative who needs some quick cash? Even holy communion is offered by some televangelists! A sacrament designed to underscore the reality of Christ in the life of his body has been transformed into another media gimmick, creating the illusion that I enjoy the fellowship of those to whom I am not accountable—indeed, who I have never met.

The most tragic example of this media interference with community is the effort on the part of some of the larger teleministries to set up satellite "churches" in which the televangelist becomes the pastor of one's local church via satellite technology.

A Present without a Past

Earlier, I mentioned the importance of context. Not only do we need a sense of belonging to a body or community of saints in this generation; we also need a sense of being a part of the holy catholic church, that is, the communion of saints from Abraham to the present.

Christianity is a historical religion. It is not escapist. It does not offer a drama of people thrown into a metaphysical struggle between time and eternity, faith and history, this world and the next. We belong in this world, although its present condition makes us, in a very real sense, aliens. Much of modern evangelicalism places us in an overly antagonistic relationship with the world. Being a part of a historical civilization or culture is often viewed as unworthy of our heavenly citizenship.

God has always considered this physical world his stage. He has placed us in this environment (by creation), preserves us through history in this environment (by providence), and saves us in this environment (by redemption). We are not saved from this world, but in this world.

The sense of alienation from this world among many evangelicals has produced not only an anti-intellectual and antisocial but an antihistorical outlook as well. The past does not matter, since "Jesus is coming soon." How interesting can church history be when we are the "terminal generation" awaiting "the great escape" from "the late great planet earth"? Nevertheless, God has been saving his people all along in community throughout biblical and postbiblical history. We even refer to the past record as "redemptive history."

American evangelicals are much more likely to know America's founding fathers than the church fathers. We are familiar with Thomas Jefferson, Benjamin Franklin, and George Washington, but who on earth is Saint Irenaeus, or Saint John Chrysostom, or Saint Athanasius? We may have memorized lines from the Gettysburg Address, but can we say the creed? The former president of the United Nations Security Council and General Assembly, Charles Malik, a member of the Orthodox Church, makes the following plea to evangelicals:

> There are also some who seem to think that nothing really worth knowing happened in the Christian world between St. Paul and Billy Graham. . . . Jesus Christ, who is the light of the world, will not be revealed as such, and His wonderful light will not shine in the aweful darkness of our world, until the American Evangelicals, on whom so much depends today, integrate into themselves, and get themselves integrated into, the unity and continuity of the cumulative Christian tradition He has shone on many a soul and many a culture in the past, and not only on the Evangelicals of today.[11]

When we say we belong to "the holy catholic church" (the Apostles' Creed), we are saying that we are heirs, spiritual descendants, of Abraham, Isaac, and Jacob, David, the apostles, Augustine, Athanasius, and Aquinas, Luther, Calvin, the Puritans, Edwards, Whitefield and Wesley, Spurgeon, Warfield, and our contemporary witnesses to Christ, with whom we are granted the distinguished title *joint-heirs*. Whether we acknowledge it, we are members not of independent churches, but of a historic communion of saints.

The "no creed but Christ" mentality of revivalistic evangelicalism contributed a great deal to the antihistorical mentality. To a large degree, it shaped American culture in that regard. Reggae singer Ziggy Marley confronts this tendency, addressing Americans, "Tomorrow people, where is your past? Tomorrow people, how long will you last? How can you have a future if you don't have a past?"

The long-running situation comedy of the 1980s, *Family Ties*, produced a movie titled, suitably, *Family Ties Vacation*. The family decided to take a trip to England, since Alex was to study for two weeks at Oxford. Alex's roommate, a lord by title, fell in love with Mallory, Alex's somewhat shallow but attractive sister. Lord William took Mallory to the five-hundred-year-old chapel at his country home. "In all the history and tradition this chapel represents," says William, "all my problems seem trivial. Here I find my place in the world." "When *I* have problems," Mallory responds, "I go shopping."

William was brought up in a culture which surrounded and nurtured him, giving him a place in this world because he had a place in history. Living for the moment (existential nihilism), illustrated in Mallory's response, stands in sharp contrast to living for the centuries—both past and future ones.

A return to community must, therefore, entail a return to Christian tradition. A generation of historically illiterate Christians can hardly revive "the faith that was once for all entrusted to the saints" (Jude 4). We must learn our past and join it, to prepare for the future.

The Tyranny of the Experts

We have delivered over our lives to experts. Life has become so complicated and technology has made everything seem so simple. Jeffrey M. Masson was once a respected psychoanalyst—projects director for the Sigmund Freud Archives. Yet, he resigned to spend the rest of his life debunking the profession. "I believe," he has said on many occasions, "psychotherapy, of any kind, is wrong."[12] Masson began to ask himself, "Was I any better off than my so-called patients? . . . Couldn't we easily have changed places? Did I really understand 'emotional problems of living' any better than anybody else, including people who had absolutely no training or background?"[13]

In politics, many feel they have no real power, so they leave that arena to "experts" and those so-called experts leave it up to the real experts—the media packagers. Harris's polls reveal that there is a growing sense of powerlessness among Americans. After Watergate (1973), 55 percent felt "alienated from the power structure." In 1985, 56 percent of adults still felt that way, but now 60 percent think they are not a part of the system. One might say, "Everyone would say he isn't as much a part of the system as he would like." But even in the turbulent 1960s, only 29 percent expressed such a feeling of alienation.

"This sense of powerlessness," says Harris, "stems from the widespread feeling that there are two tiers of justice, privilege, and affluence—one for those who are insiders [experts] in Washington, Wall Street, corporate America, and major institutions across the nation, and another for ordinary citizens."[14]

In 1966, Americans (particularly the younger ones) were at odds with the system, but they felt a part of it—only 26 percent thought "the people running the country don't really care what happens to me," compared to 55 percent a decade later. "As an isolated individual," the pollster comments, "it is not hard to feel a sense of remoteness from those who are running the leading institutions today."[15] Harris concludes, "The price that might be paid if the alienated ever became openly hostile could be enormous. . . . The trouble is that no one really knows what the breaking point might be. . . . But when 100 million American adults say they feel alienated from the establishment leadership, a national condition exists that cannot continue to be ignored."[16]

We even turn our emotional security over to experts. We pay a "professional" two hundred dollars an hour to listen to us and to tell us what very often our pastor, parent, friend, or neighbor could have advised. That is how desperate we have become in the absence of community. Harris notes, "It is obviously difficult at best" in our therapeutic, individualistic, materialistic age "to feel a sense of having deep roots, of belonging, and of making a contribution to the larger community in which one lives."[17]

During this past Thanksgiving I decided not to go home, since there was so much to be done. I took for granted that I would be cared for and generously fed by someone in our church—a number of people were inviting "strays" into their homes for dinner. As I was driving to Dave and Jodi Hansen's for Thanksgiving, I happened to tune into a Christian radio station. A Christian psychiatrist was taking calls. "How are you going to manage this holiday season?" he asked. The calls came in one after the other. Here are people, I thought to myself, who are going home, for Thanksgiving, calling a stranger for advice on how to enjoy their family. Meanwhile, I wasn't even going home and yet I felt perfectly secure, comfortable, and relaxed on my way to Dave and Jodi's. I'm sure there are churches like this across this land, but there are too many people (Christian people) calling in to the therapeutic talk shows to suggest that either the church or the family is providing meaningful community and, hence, psychological security.

Relativism

"People pick and choose truths," says Marty, "as if on a cafeteria line, until they get the right diet or mixture." To select the desired ingredients, "you 'drop in' casually at the church of your choice. It is not a natural community of believers so much as an expression of the individual self according to the accidents of locale or economic position.

The supportive faith of a community beyond the local congregation is forgotten."[18]

Evangelicals want unity, but with theological ambiguity (the euphemism *diversity* is often employed). To be sure, we need ethnic, cultural, educational, and socioeconomic diversity. And there is no reason why Christians have to agree on every doctrinal point. But that statement has often been enlarged to mean that Christians need not find, establish, discover, root their unity in creedal or confessional commitment.

Community requires, more than anything else, a common set of beliefs. Communists may have had their own internal disputes, but their dedication to Marxist-Leninist dogma made them comrades to the bitter end. Islam is a formidable cultural, sociopolitical force because its adherents are relentless in both their conviction and application of Islamic doctrine. Modern evangelicalism appears to be the only metaphysical system in which unity is based on common experiences, vocabulary, and rituals instead of theological convictions or philosophical systems.

Until we become serious about the content of our faith, sectarian strife will continue to cripple the Christian cause. The great truths of historic, biblical Christianity make one forget his or her sectarian eccentricities and join the larger team.

Regaining Confidence in the Institutional Church

Earlier, I pointed out the staggering lack of confidence the average American has in the church. Of course, the deterioration of respect for the local church has its roots in the trends we have described. Nevertheless, more than cultural influences must share the blame. We must ask ourselves or, better yet, ask the unchurched public why they have such a cynical attitude toward the church. First, professing Christians, laypeople, share the blame. Whatever is wrong with the church today, it is still the ordained com munity, the kingdom of God. We do not abandon the family when it has fallen on hard times; we improve it. A Roman Catholic priest, Father James Fehren, defends the parish (local church). "Although some people think," he says, "that the parish is about to perish, that it is an outmoded institution, that it is a structure which does not reflect the sense of community we hear so much about today," it is God's ordained community. God did not ordain Bible study, quiet time, or discipleship, prayer, or accountability groups. That is not to say that such groups are unnecessary—just that they are not, in God's estimation, the Christian's home. Father Fehren notes that many Catholics (like many Protestants) "want to be free to float wherever they please for any sacrament, desert their own parishes and run off to any one which happens to please their cultural, aesthetic, or spiritual palates and have no ties to the parishes in which they live." Nevertheless, says Fehren, "two thousand years of experience has taught us that we need the parish. The parish is often the church in miniature and Christ is the heart of each parish."

It used to be that leaving the neighborhood church for reasons other than a family move constituted a great offense. To leave one's church meant that the parish had become so biblically unsound that reform was impossible. Of course, the transience of modern society accounts for a great deal of instability—we're always moving somewhere else—but many people move from church to church without ever changing homes. We have become consumer-oriented: Instead of assessing the church for its commitment to the Scriptures and evangelical piety, we shop for a church much the way we shop for a favorite restaurant.

And the electronic church doesn't help in this regard. Marty catches the contradiction:

> Late Saturday night Mr. and Mrs. Invisible Religion get their jollies from the ruffled-shirted, pink-tuxedoed men and the high-coiffured, low-necklined celebrity women who talk about themselves under the guise of Born Again autobiogra-

phies. Sunday morning the watchers get their jollies as Holy
Ghost entertainers caress microphones among spurting
fountains and a highly professional . . . leader entertains
them. Are they to turn off that very set and then make their
way down the block to a congregation of real believers, sinners, offkey choirs, and sweaty and homely people who
need them, people they do not like but are supposed to
love, ordinary pastors who preach grace and calls to discipleship, pleas for stewardship that do not come well-oiled?
Never. Well, hardly ever.[20]

Second, there is the failure of the institutional leadership.
George Gallup, Jr., is recognized as the nation's pollster and
his study of America's faith offers a few reasons for the
hightened cynicism about the church.

The first reason is the superficiality and shallowness of the
church. "The leaders are afraid of theology," said one poll
respondent, an executive in southern California. "I think the
churches have gotten like a lot of parts of society," he continued. "They have to worry so much about paying the rent
that they have forgotten the good news. They forget the
evangelical message." The executive concludes, "I find some
of the clergy are very wonderful people, but a lot of them
have to seek out the almighty dollar so much that they are
robbing the people of the great heritage of the Church."[21]

Gallup also interviewed a Navy officer who served
Vietnam. The officer "recalled his youth as a flower child
and his feeling that his church life gave him no perspective
on the problems he faced nor a world-view to deal with the
war when it came." The officer said, "The cathedrals and
the foreign missionaries are nice, but the Church has gotten
to be a kind of power broker. That is not religion."[22] And so
it isn't. Many have turned either from or against the institutional church because it has turned aside from its
prophetic and redeeming mission.

Gallup notes, after extensive surveys, "There is great
hunger among the churched as well as the unchurched for
a sharper focus on the primary questions of life."[23]

Why would the churched have a hunger for theological

depth and understanding of life's meaning similar to the unchurched? And can this lack of substance be responsible for much of the apathy? As much as 49 percent of the unchurched believed that "most churches and synagogues today are not effective in helping people find meaning in life." But even more remarkable is the fact that 39 percent of the churched felt that way, too—only a 10-percent difference! Similarly, 56 percent of the unchurched are convinced that "most churches and synagogues today are too concerned with organizational as opposed to theological or spiritual issues." "Church members," said Gallup, "agreed by 47 percent."[24] Only a 9-percent difference there!

Clearly, something is wrong with the emphasis of our preaching, teaching, outreach, and activity. We think the people want more programs, but, judging by their own responses, they really want more meat. "The negative attitude of young people toward organized religion," says Gallup, includes the complaint of "the shallow and superficial stance of so many church members; the inability of congregations to deal with the basics of faith and appeal to youth on a solid spiritual basis."[25] Father Fehren adds, "To know Scripture and theology and to present Christ to the people" are the minister's responsibility.[26] We cannot expect the laity to grow or stay if the clergy are apathetic or ignorant in their preaching or teaching ministry.

A second issue is secularization. According to the general public, "their heavenly hopes are far from fulfilled in the earthbound churches."[27] The unchurched do indeed want to see a church that confronts society in enlightening rather than predictable, uninspired ways. It's not that they want the church to isolate its interests to exclusively pastoral concerns. In fact, "younger saints," says Gallup, "are always given the dreadful assignment of letting the people in charge have the bad news: they are out of touch with God and their world is filled with disharmony, insensitivity, and injustice."[28]

The public, particularly the younger generation, is looking for a church that is in touch with God—that is, familiar with his attributes, his way of doing things, his activity in the past and his objectives for the future. And they want that God-centered church to then speak effectively to the pressing issues of their time—all of them, at bottom, spiritual issues. They do not want an echo of the secular establishment (either the left or the right), but something different. They want an eternal perspective on temporal issues, and the church generally, in their estimation, does not provide this. Gallup observes, "Young people in America are vitally concerned about their religious faith. Some of this concern translates into sharp, persistent criticism of the institutional church for its failure to match up to its message."[29]

Gallup insists that "people are surprised, alarmed, and resentful that the churches are not taking seriously this God-given responsibility and instead wander off on secondary pursuits and superficial outings, and are unwilling to participate, sustain, and support those religious communities that live and teach a high noble calling and practice what they preach."[30]

People resent million-dollar campaigns against a second-rate film on Christ's "last temptation." Certainly the movie was blasphemous and historically untrue, but that's not the point. I found it somewhat ironic that Trinity Broadcasting Network (TBN) spearheaded a major protest of the film studio while its leadership denies the biblical, classical, orthodox positions with regard to the person of Christ! The general public wonders how biblically and theologically illiterate people could "wander off into secondary pursuits" while God's "people are destroyed from lack of knowledge" (Hos. 4:6).

Harry Blamires insists that secularization is due to the loss of the Christian mind. We go to church, pray, engage in devotions, and appear outwardly devout, but we think like pagans. Because "this world is not my home," the tendency is to ignore the reality of this world and its relationship to the believer. We narrowly define our spiritual life in terms of praying, reading the Bible (as a devotional guide), and participating in religious activities.

The public is seeking what is no more than a biblical view of the church—a community of believers who take the church into the world by occupying their outposts in their vocations, in their families, and in their neighborhoods.

If the public wants the church to get involved in society, does that mean it wants the church to lose its spiritual zeal? Hardly. They want the church to be in the world, but not of it. Even unbelievers want to see the church live up to its own message and mission.

A Dayton, Ohio, study, found that the humanitarian impulse of many young people "appears to be fueled by their valuing a Christian orientation which they believe the church to have neglected or given a rather low priority."[31] In other words, many young people have discovered that Christianity is more concerned about the plight of the homeless, the environment, and the value of human life than is the contemporary church, generally speaking. This weakness, says Gallup, is not perceived as an overemphasis on the eternal, for the churches are also charged with being earthbound. Rather, it is the churches' spiritual apathy, matched by their "excessive materialism and hypocritical stance," that is responsible for their failure to offer solutions to such social crises.[32]

But, again, the people, especially the young people, are weary of secular, worldly solutions. A young Presbyterian in the Dayton survey remarked, "The Church is worried about the condition of the world and not worried about its own people; it tries to save the world while people in the Church go to hell."[33] The social gospel of the right has taken over where the social gospel of the left had exhausted itself. Many of the conservative churches, once apathetic toward world conditions, are now so busy baptizing the conservative political establishment that the eternal perspective has been lost.

Many people are disappointed by the divorce between personal and public piety. They want the church to be involved with this world, but in a way that spiritualizes the secular rather than secularizing the spiritual. They believe that Christianity offers eternal hope for this world's immediate needs, but are not convinced the modern church agrees.

A third issue is legalism. Afraid of the world, many churches, according to Marty, are "fencing [young people] in with rules and regulations, and maybe even separating them with physical distance from the larger society."[34] A further cause of alienation from the local church and of the churches' failure to offer deeper meaning is legalism, according to Gallup. "Narrowness may be interpreted in such practices as strict dress codes: opposition to social dancing, use of alcoholic beverages . . . and all kinds of smoking; censure of profanity, participation in public amusement—especially motion pictures and legitimate theater. This kind of religious world," Gallup says, "is presently rejected by many within the ranks of the unchurched."[35] And that is all right, since that kind of religious world was rejected by Jesus Christ almost two thousand years ago. Our job is to bring the churches into line with the church Jesus founded.

When churches add to the Scriptures in either doctrine or practice, biblical Christianity is invariably rejected along with the impossible and unlivable accessories. Such forms of religion trivialize truth and, by raising opinion to the level of Scripture (as in medieval Rome), fundamentalist churches often weaken biblical authority.

Churches often impose restrictions for the purpose of inculcating a sense of community. Many conservative religious colleges and other institutions are bent on creating a monastic community in which Christian liberty is sacrificed for group identity. But when that group identity is more restrictive than the biblical blueprint, a genuine sense of community is lost.

It must be recognized, then, that real community can be expressed only as people are centered around biblical faith and practice. Cults appeal to those who would be dominated. Many young people today crave authority and would like to have a guru dictate to them, but a genuinely Christian community will seek to engender self-control, responsibility, and freedom among its believers. A community is a voluntary association of those who hold certain things in common. A forced or restrictive community is actually a prison.

Many of the unchurched, then, might be more attracted to the local Christian community if it evidenced a serious posture toward truth, if it gave meaning and purpose to daily living, if it provided an eternal perspective for human problems, and if it were not so legalistic. Perhaps these people would even appreciate the church telling them forthrightly that the term *unchurched Christian* is an oxymoron; that genuine Christians follow the pattern of the earliest disciples who "devoted themselves to the apostles teaching and to the fellowship, to the breaking of bread and to prayer" (Acts 2:42). At first, the suggestion that individualistic Christianity is not an option might offend their democratic sensitivities, but we can be sure they will at least thank us for being honest and for having the courage of our convictions. That is more than they are willing to say about the local church at present.

Conclusion

The church was once the center of the neighborhood. It held the larger community together. The chapel was always built at the center of the university campus. Business relationships had to conform to the standards of brotherhood established and demonstrated by the local church. Of course, that was when the body politic was also the visible body of Christ.

During the "rain of the gods" in Western culture, Christianity has become one of many voices. If it produces spectacular crusades, rallies, television shows, international ministries, and entertaining superchurches, but cannot give alienated, isolated selves a home, a community with tradition and a connection with the wider gathering of saints, its cheerful arenas and state-of-the-art cameras will one day be sold to another band of gypsies. If, by rediscovering the "faith [its truths, its traditions] once and for all delivered unto the saints," we can become humble centers of simple faith and piety, we will have restored more visibly the communion of the saints.

Notes

Introduction

1. Hans Christian Anderson, "The Emperor's New Clothes."

2. Francis A. Schaeffer, *The Church at the End of the Twentieth Century: The Church before the Watching World* (Westchester, Ill.: Crossway, 1985), 39.

3. George Marsden, ed., *Evangelicalism and Modern America* (Grand Rapids: Eerdmans, 1984), xiv.

4. George Barna and William P. McKay, *Vital Signs: Emerging Social Trends and the Future of American Christianity* (Westchester, Ill.: Crossway, 1984), 4.

5. Louis Harris, *Inside America* (New York: Vintage, 1987), 268.

6. Oxford Analytica Editors, *America in Perspective* (New York: Houghton Mifflin, 1986), 115.

7. Martin E. Marty, *The Pro and Con Book of Religious America: A Bicentennial Argument* (Waco: Word, 1975), 17, 25.

8. Donald G. Bloesch, *Crumbling Foundations: Death and Rebirth in an Age of Upheaval* (Grand Rapids: Zondervan, 1984), 110.

9. Ibid.

Chapter 1

1. Harvey Cox, *Religion in the Secular City: Toward a Postmodern Theology* (New York: Simon and Schuster, 1984), 200.

2. John W. Whitehead, *The Stealing of America* (Westchester, Ill.: Crossway, 1983).

3. Cotton Mather, *Magnalia Christi Americana* (reprint; New York: Unger, 1970), 39.

4. C. S. Lewis, *Studies in Medieval and Renaissance Studies*, "Edmund Spenser" (Oxford: Oxford University Press, 1954), 121–22.

5. John Calvin, *Institutes of the Christian Religion*, ed. John T. McNeill, trans. Ford Lewis Battles (Philadelphia: Westminster, 1960), 2 vols., 4.1.7, 8.

189

6. Joseph Conforti, *Samuel Hopkins and the New Divinity Movement: Calvinism, the Congregational Ministry, and Reform in New England Between the Great Awakenings* (Grand Rapids: Eerdmans, 1981), 1.

7. Mather, *Magnolia Christi Americana*, 108.

8. Peter Gay, *The Enlightenment: An Interpretation*, vol. 1, *The Rise of Modern Paganism* (New York: Norton, 1966), 299. This immensely popular secular treatment provides many helpful insights, though at times its style exaggerates the content.

9. Richard Hofstadter, *America at 1750: A Social History* (New York: Vintage, 1973), 228–29.

10. Conforti, *Samuel Hopkins*, 62.

11. Richard Hofstadter, *Anti-Intellectualism in American Life* (New York: Vintage, 1963), 59ff. In this book the author recognizes that the best days of America's intellectual life were at the beginning, with the Puritans, and nothing has replaced that religious culture. Stern words for the role of popular evangelicalism in anti-intellectualism are supported by ample sources.

12. Ibid.

13. Quoted by Hofstadter, ibid.

14. Ibid.

15. Will Herberg, *Intercollegiate Review* 5, 2 (1968–69).

16. From Andre Maurois's introduction to *Candide* (New York: Bantam, 1959), 1.

17. Ibid.

18. Ibid., 6.

19. William Warren Sweet, *Religion in the Development of American Culture: 1765–1840* (New York: Charles Scribner's Sons), preface.

20. Ibid.

21. Michael Harrington, *The Politics at God's Funeral: The Spiritual Crisis of Western Civilization* (New York: Penguin, 1983), 12.

22. Quoted in Friedrich Nietzsche, *Schopenhauer As Educator*, trans. J. W. Hillesheim (reprint; Chicago: Regnery, Gateway Editions, 1965), 37.

23. Hofstadter, *America at 1750*, 244.

24. Ibid., 247.

25. Ibid., 252.

26. Gerald R. Cragg, *The Church and the Age of Reason* (1961; New York: Penguin, 1985), 145.

27. Hofstadter, *America at 1750*, 272.

28. Arthur Schlesinger, Jr., *Cycles of American History* (New York: Houghton Mifflin, 1986), 5.

29. Hofstadter, *Anti-Intellectualism in American Life*, 86–87.

30. Ibid., 83.

31. Robert N. Bellah, et.al., *The Habits of the Heart: Individualism and Commitment in American Life* (New York: Harper and Row, 1986), 84.

32. Ibid., 220.

33. George Gallup, Jr., and Jim Castelli, *The People's Religion* (New York: Macmillan, 1990), 48.

34. Ibid.

35. John T. McNeill, *The History and Character of Calvinism* (Oxford: Oxford University Press, 1954), 425.

36. Ibid., 426.

37. Mark A. Noll, Nathan Hatch, and George Marsden, *The Search for Christian America* (Westchester, Ill.: Crossway, 1983), 118.

38. Cox, *Religion in the Secular City*, 200.

39. Quoted in Garth Lean and Sir Arnold Lunn, *The Christian Counter-Attack* (New Rochelle, N.Y.: Arlington House, 1969), 18.

40. Christopher Lasch, *The Culture of Narcissism* (New York: Warner, 1979), 25.

41. Joseph Haroutunian, *Piety versus Moralism: The Passing of New England Theology* (New York: Harper and Sons, 1932), 145.

42. Jerry Falwell. *Listen America* (New York: Doubleday, 1980), 50.

43. Hofstadter, *Anti-Intellectualism in American Life*, 89.

44. Quoted in Noll, Hatch, and Marsden, *The Search for Christian America*, 131.

45. Gallup and Castelli, *The People's Religion*, 60.

46. Sydney Ahlstrom, "From Puritanism to Evangelicalism," in *The Evangelicals: What They Believe, Who They Are, Where They Are Changing*, ed. John D. Woodbridge and David F. Wells (Nashville: Abingdon, 1975), 288.

47. Haroutunian, *Piety versus Moralism*, xxxiii.

48. Mark Hatfield, *Between a Rock and a Hard Place* (Waco: Word, 1976), 101.

Chapter 2

1. Allan Bloom, *The Closing of the American Mind: Education and the Crisis of Reason* (New York: Simon and Schuster, 1987),.42.

2. Robert N. Bellah, et. al., *The Habits of the Heart: Individualism and Commitment in American Life* (New York: Harper and Row, 1986), 293.

3. Richard Hofstadter, *Anti-Intellectualism in American Life* (New York: Vintage, 1963), 55.

4. Charles Finney, *Lectures on Revival*.

5. Stephen Berk, *Calvinism versus Democracy: Timothy Dwight and the Origins of American Evangelical Orthodoxy* (Berkley: University of California Press, 1968), x.

6. Ibid., xii.

7. Ibid., 12.

8. Mark A. Noll, Nathan Hatch, and George Marsden, *The Search for Christian America* (Westchester, Ill.: Crossway, 1983), 118–19.

9. Berk, *Calvinism versus Democracy*, 59–61.

10. Hofstadter, *Anti-Intellectualism in American Life*, 97.

11. Charles Finney, *Systematic Theology* (reprint; Minneapolis: Bethany, 1976). Foreword by Henry Conn.

12. Ibid.

13. Ibid.

14. Quoted in William Mc Loughlin, *Billy Sunday Was His Real Name* (Chicago: University of Chicago Press, 1955), 158.

15. George Marsden, *Fundamentalism in American Culture* (Oxford: Oxford University Press, 1985), 35.

16. Quoted in Hofstadter, *Anti-Intellectualism in American Life*, 115.

17. Quoted in Sidney E. Mead, *The Lively Experiment: The Shaping of Christianity in America* (New York: Harper and Row, 1963), 114–15.

18. Martin E. Marty, *The Pro and Con Book of Religious America: A Bicentennial Argument* (Waco: Word, 1975), 43.

19. Pat Robertson, *The Secret Kingdom: A Promise of Hope and Freedom in a World of Turmoil* (Nashville: Nelson, 1983), 59, 66–67.

20. Ibid., 78.

21. William James, *Pragmatism* (reprint; New York: Meridian, 1955), 192–95.

22. Oxford Analytica Editors, *America in Perspective* (New York: Houghton Mifflin, 1986), 128.

23. James Davison Hunter, *Evangelicalism: The Coming Generation* (Chicago: University of Chicago Press, 1987), see esp. chap. 3.

24. Marty, *Pro and Con Book*, 43.

25. Robert Schuller, introduction to Paul Yonggi Cho, *The Fourth Dimension* (Plainfield, N. J.: Logos, 1979).

Chapter 3

1. Richard Hofstadter, *Anti-Intellectualism in American Life* (New York: Vintage, 1963), 85ff.

2. Ibid., 115.

3. Charles Finney, *Lectures on Revival*, quoted in Richard Hofstadter, *Anti-Intellectualism in American Life* (New York: Vintage, 1973), 109.

4. Ibid.

5. Gregory Lewis, *Is God for Sale?* (Wheaton: Tyndale, 1979), 16.

6. *Christianity Today*, March 5, 1990.

7. A. W. Tozer, *The New Cross*.

Chapter 4

1. R. Emmett Tyrrell, Jr., ed., *Orthodoxy: The American Spectator's Twentieth Anniversary Anthology* (New York: Harper and Row, 1987), 131.

2. Colin Campbell, *The Romantic Ethic and the Spirit of Modern Consumerism* (Oxford: Basil Blackwell, 1987), 101.

3. Ibid.

4. Ibid., 109.

5. Carl F. H. Henry, *The Los Angeles Times*.

6. George Barna and William P. McKay, *Vital Signs: Emerging Social Trends and the Future of American Christianity* (Westchester, Ill.: Crossway, 1984), 140.

7. Ibid., 141.

8. Garry Wills, *Reagan's America* (New York: Penguin, 1988), 235.

9. Ibid., 237.

10. Christopher Lasch, *The Culture of Narcissism* (New York: Warner, 1979), 62.

11. Robert Schuller, *Self-Esteem: The New Reformation* (Waco: Word, 1982), 98ff.

12. Lasch, *Culture of Narcissism*, 21.

13. Louis Harris, *Inside America* (New York: Vintage, 1987), 3.

14. Lasch, *Culture of Narcissism*, 29.

15. Robert N. Bellah, et. al., *The Habits of the Heart: Individualism and Commitment in American Life* (New York: Harper and Row, 1985), 65.

16. Schuller, *Self-Esteem*, 64.

17. Ibid., 14.

18. Ibid., 80.

19. Ibid., 27.

20. Ibid., 99.

21. Ibid.

22. Lester Sumrall, *The Will* (South Bend, Ind.: Le Sea, 1985), 61.

23. Morris Cerillo, fund-raising appeal.

24. Kenneth Copeland, "The Force of Love," tape BCC–56 (Fort Worth: Kenneth Copeland Ministries).

25. Robert Schuller, *Peace of Mind Through Possibility Thinking* (Old Tappan, N.J.: Revell, 1977), 131–32.

26. Kenneth Copeland, crusade tape, July 19, 1987.

27. Martin Luther, *The Bondage of the Will* (reprint; Grand Rapids: Baker, 1976), 36.

28. Krister Stendahl, in Martin E. Marty, *The Pro and Con Book of Religious America: A Bicentennial Argument* (Waco: Word, 1975), 39.

29. Ibid.

30. *A Reformation Debate: John Calvin and Jacopo Sadoleto*, ed. John C. Olin (reprint; Grand Rapids: Baker, 1976), 58.

31. Bellah, et. al., *Habits of the Heart*, 109.

32. Thomas Constable, "The Gospel Message," in *A Tribute to John Walvoord*, ed. Donald K. Campbell (Chicago: Moody 1982), 209.

33. Bellah, et. al., *Habits of the Heart*, 232.

34. Louis Schneider and Sanford M. Dornbusch, *Popular Religion: Inspirational Books in America* (Chicago: University of Chicago Press,1958), jacket.

35. Ibid., 43.

36. Ibid., 47.

37. Ibid., 75.

38. Elton Trueblood, *The Life We Prize* (New York: Harper and Brothers, 1951), 45.

39. Barna and McKay, *Vital Signs*, 142.

40. Gloria Copeland, *God's Will Is Prosperity* (Fort Worth: Kenneth Copeland Ministries, 1983), 12.

41. Kenneth Hagin, *Faith Food for Winter* (Tulsa: Kenneth Hagin Ministries), 58.

42. Gloria Copeland, *God's Will Is Prosperity*, 13.

43. Kenneth Copeland, *Laws of Prosperity* (Fort Worth: Kenneth Copeland Ministries), 57.

44. Ibid., 98.

45. Barna and McKay, *Vital Signs*, 141.

46. Marty, *Pro and Con Book*, 21–22.

Chapter 5

1. James Davison Hunter, *Evangelicalism: The Coming Generation* (Chicago: University of Chicago Press, 1987), 46–47.

2. Alexis de Tocqueville, *Democracy in America*, ed. J. P. Mayer, trans. George Lawrence (New York: Harper and Row, 1988), 429.

3. *Webster's Dictionary for Everyday Use* (Baltimore: Ottenheimer, 1981).

4. Quoted in Martin E. Marty, *Pilgrims in Their Own Land: Five Hundred Years of Religion in America* (New York: Penguin, 1984).

5. Richard Hofstadter, *Anti-Intellectualism in American Life* (New York: Vintage, 1963), 79.

6. Bernard Reardon, *Religion in the Age of Romanticism* (Cambridge: Cambridge University Press, 1985), vii.

7. Ibid., 9.

8. There is an inherent Gnosticism in American Protestantism, even beyond the sect-consciousness, which is wholly antithetical to the larger Protestant Reformation tradition. See Philip Lee's *Against the Protestant Gnostics* (Oxford: Oxford University Press, 1986) for an excellent treatment.

9. C. Gregg Singer, *A Theological Interpretation of American History* (Nutley, N.J.: Craig, 1978), 40–41.

10. For a broader background to this radical mystical tendency, see Ronald Knox's outstanding work, *Enthusiasm* (Oxford: Oxford University Press, 1959).

11. Mark A. Noll, Nathan Hatch, and George Marsden, *The Search for Christian America* (Westchester, Ill.: Crossway, 1983).

12. Nietzsche, quoted in Michael Harrington, *The Politics at God's Funeral: The Spiritual Crisis of Western Civilization* (New York: Penguin, 1983), 35.

13. Ibid., 35.

14. Jackson Lears, *No Place for Grace: Antimodernism and the Transformation of American Culture, 1880–1920* (New York: Pantheon, 1981), 32.

15. Walter A. Elwell, ed., *Evangelical Dictionary of Theology* (Grand Rapids: Baker, 1984), 856.

16. Ibid., 857.

17. Harrington, *Politics at God's Funeral*, 14.

18. See Immanuel Kant's *Critique of Pure Reason* (reprint; New York: Everyman, 1945), preface.

19. Elwell, ed., *Evangelical Dictionary of Theology*, 981.

20. Reardon, *Religion in the Age of Romanticism*, 56.

21. Martin E. Marty, The *Pro and Con Book of Religious America: A Bicentennial Argument* (Waco: Word, 1975), 118.

22. Ibid., 115.

23. Quoted in Garth Lean and Sir Arnold Lunn, *The Christian Counter-Attack* (New Rochelle, N.Y.: Arlington House, 1969), 102.

24. Marty, *Pro and Con Book*, 119.

25. Harvey Cox, *Religion in the Secular City: Toward a Postmodern Theology* (New York: Simon and Schuster, 1984), 200.

26. Noll, Hatch, and Marsden, *Search for Christian America*, 43.

27. Quoted in Harrington, *Politics at God's Funeral*, 58.

28. Colin Wilson, *The New Existentialism* (Hounslow, Middlesex: Wildwood House, 1980), 33.

Chapter 6

1. Michael Harrington, *The Politics at God's Funeral: The Spiritual Crisis of Western Civilization* (New York: Penguin, 1983), 35.

2. Ibid.

3. The Stanford Research Institute is devoted to the exploration and promotion of New Age concepts (see Marilyn Ferguson's *Aquarian Conspiracy: Personal and Social Transformation in the 1980s* [New York: St. Martin's, 1987]).

4. Ferguson, *Aquarian Conspiracy*, 120.

5. Ibid., 19.

6. Kenneth Copeland, "The Force of Love," tape BCC–56 (Fort Worth: Kenneth Copeland Ministries).

7. Kenneth Hagin, *Word of Faith*, December 1980, 14.

8. Christopher Lasch, *The Culture of Narcissism* (New York: Warner, 1979), 31.

9. Ibid., 32.

10. See Lewis Sperry Chafer's *He That Is Spiritual* (1918; Grand Rapids: Zondervan, 1967).

11. Ferguson, *Aquarian Conspiracy*, 47.

12. Ibid., 48.

13. Lewis Schneider and Sanford M. Dornbusch, *Popular Religion: Inspirational Books in America* (Chicago: University of Chicago Press, 1958), 60.

14. Georgia Harkness, *Prayer and the Common Life* (New York: Abingdon-Cokesbury, 1948), 66, 167.

15. Pat Robertson, *The Secret Kingdom: A Promise of Hope and Freedom in a World of Turmoil* (Nashville: Nelson, 1987), 73.

16. Ibid.

17. Ibid., 83.

18. Ibid., 222.

19. Henry David Thoreau, *On Man and Nature* (reprint; New York: Peter Pauper, 1960), 15.

20. Ibid., 18.

21. Ibid., 19.

22. Ibid., 25.

23. See D. R. McConnell's *A Different Gospel* (Peabody, Mass.: Hendrickson, 1988).

24. Paul Yonggi Cho, *The Fourth Dimension: The Key to Putting Your Faith to Work for a Successful Life* (Plainfield, N.J.: Logos, 1980), 44.

25. Ibid., 83.

26. Earl Paulk, *The Unity of Faith* (Decatur, Ga.: Chapel Hill Harvester, 1987), 4.

27. Donald G. Bloesch, *Crumbling Foundations: Death and Rebirth in an Age of Upheaval* (Grand Rapids: Zondervan, 1984), 77.

28. Dave Hunt and T. A. McMahon, *Seduction of Christianity* (Eugene, Ore.: Harvest House, 1985), 153.

29. Ibid., 154.

30. Bloesch, *Crumbling Foundations*, 87.

31. Pat Robertson and William Proctor, *Beyond Reason: How Miracles Can Change Your Life* (New York: Morrow, 1987), 108.

32. B. B. Warfield, *Studies in Perfectionism* (reprint; Nutley, N.J.: Presbyterian and Reformed, 1958).

33. Richard Rice, *God's Foreknowledge and Man's Free Will* (Minneapolis: Bethany, 1985), 10.

34. Ibid., 11.

35. Ibid., 22.

36. *Christianity Today*, February 19, 1990.

37. Ferguson, *Aquarian Conspiracy*, 70.

38. Roshi Philip Kapleau, *Zen Dawn in the West* (London: Rider, 1987), 12.

39. Arthur M. Young, *The Reflexive Universe: Evolution of Consciousness* (Mill Valley, Calif.: Rob Briggs, 1984), 385.

40. Ferguson, *Aquarian Conspiracy*, 30.

41. Kenneth Copeland, *Believer's Voice of Victory*, 1982, 2.

42. Eric Voegelin, *Science, Politics, and Gnosticism*, trans. W. J. Fitzpatrick (Chicago: Regnery, Gateway Editions, 1968), 9.

43. Viktor Frankl, *Psychotherapy and Existentialism* (New York: Simon and Schuster, 1974), 71.

44. Roshi, *Zen Dawn in the West*, 10.

45. Lasch, *Culture of Narcissism*, 33.

46. Harvey Cox, *Religion in the Secular City: Toward a Postmodern Theology* (New York: Simon and Schuster, 1984), 209.

47. Lasch, *Culture of Narcissism*, 43.

48. Ferguson, *Aquarian Conspiracy*, 29.

49. Lasch, *Culture of Narcissism*, 46.

50. Roshi, *Zen Dawn in the West*, 26.

51. Ibid., 27.

52. Ibid., 26.

53. George Gallup, Jr., and Jim Castelli, *The People's Religion* (New York: Macmillan, 1990), 367.

54. George Gallup, Jr., and David Poling, *The Search for America's Faith* (Nashville: Abingdon, 1980), 20.

55. Ibid., 18.

56. Quoted in Ferguson, *Aquarian Conspiracy*, 268.

57. Ibid., 371.

Chapter 7

1. Martin E. Marty, *Pilgrims in Their Own Land: Five Hundred Years of Religion in America* (New York: Penguin, 1984), 316.

2. Quoted in Richard Hofstadter, *Anti-Intellectualism in American Life* (New York: Viking, 1963), 108.

3. Francis A. Schaeffer, *Complete Works of Francis Schaeffer*, vol. 4 (Westchester, Ill.: Crossway, 1982), 31.

4. Ibid., 32.

5. Donald G. Bloesch, *Crumbling Foundations: Death and Rebirth in an Age of Upheaval* (Grand Rapids: Zondervan, 1984), 21–22.

6. St. John de Crevecoeur, *Letters from an American Farmer* (reprint; New York: 1957), 44–47.

7. Hofstadter, *Anti-Intellectualism in American Life*, 85.

8. "Science Can't Provide Ultimate Answers," *U.S. News and World Report*, February 1985.

9. Allan Bloom, *The Closing of the American Mind: Education and the Crisis of Reason* (New York: Simon and Schuster, 1987), 25–26.

10. Christopher Lasch, *The Culture of Narcissism* (New York: Warner, 1979), 259.

11. Ibid., 223.

12. *USA TODAY*, June 28, 1988, 1.

13. Quoted in E. D. Hirsch, Jr., *Cultural Literacy: What Every American Needs to Know* (New York: Vintage, 1988), 7.

14. Ibid., 20.

15. Martin E. Marty, *The Pro and Con Book of Religious America: A Bicentennial Argument* (Waco: Word, 1975), 40.

16. Hofstadter, *Anti-Intellectualism in American Life*, 59–60.

17. Marilyn Ferguson, *The Aquarian Conspiracy: Personal and Social Transformation in the 1980s* (New York: St. Martin's, 1987), 280.

18. Bloom, *Closing of the American Mind*, 26.

19. Lasch, *Culture of Narcissism*, 141.

20. *A Reformation Debate: John Calvin and Jacopo Sadoleto*, ed. John C. Olin (reprint; Grand Rapids: Baker, 1976), 65.

21. L. Praamsma, *The Church in the Twentieth Century*, vol. 7 (St. Catharine's, Ontario: Omega, 1975), 63.

22. Ibid.

23. Ibid.

24. Ibid.

25. James Davison Hunter, *Evangelicals: The Coming Generation* (Chicago: University of Chicago, 1987), 25.

26. Bloom, *Closing of the American Mind*, 56.

27. George Lindbeck, "The Church's Mission to a Postmodern Culture," in *Postmodern Theology*, ed. Diogenes Allen and Frederick B. Burnham (San Francisco: Harper and Row, 1989), 44–48.

28. Quoted in George Barna and William P. McKay, *Vital Signs: Emerging Social Trends and the Future of American Christianity* (Westchester, Ill.: Crossway, 1984), 110.

29. Harvey Cox, *Religion in the Secular City: Toward a Postmodern Theology* (New York: Simon and Schuster, 1987), 224.

30. Diogenes Allen, "Christian Values in a Post-Christian Context," in *Postmodern Theology*, 21.

31. T. S. Eliot, *Christianity and Culture* (reprint; New York: Harcourt Brace Jovanovich, 1977), 15.

32. Oxford Analytica Editors, *America in Perspective* (Boston: Houghton Mifflin, 1986), 179.

33. Lindbeck, "The Church's Mission," 43.

Chapter 8

1. Charles Reich, *The Greening of America: The Coming of a New Consciousness and the Rebirth of a Future* (New York: Bantam, 1971), 7.

2. Martin E. Marty, *The Pro and Con Book of Religious America: A Bicentennial Argument*, (Waco: Word, 1975), 47.

3. Ibid., 39.

4. George Gallup, Jr., and David Poling, *The Search for America's Faith* (Nashville: Abingdon, 1980), 90.

5. Louis Harris, *Inside America* (New York: Vintage, 1987), 71.

6. Ibid., 256.

7. Robert N. Bellah, et. al., *The Habits of the Heart: Individualism and Commitment in American Life* (New York: Harper and Row, 1986), 263.

8. *The Los Angeles Times*, February 1, 1984.

9. Kenneth Lipper, *Wall Street* (New York: Berkley, 1988), 18.

10. Tom Wolfe, in an interview, *Time*, February 13, 1989, 90.

11. Charles Malik, *The Two Tasks* (Westchester, Ill.: Cornerstone, 1980), 23.

12. Jeffrey M. Masson, *Against Therapy: Emotional Tyranny and the Myth of Psychological Healing* (New York: Macmillan, 1985), ix.

13. Ibid.

14. Harris, *Inside America*, 33.

15. Ibid., 37.

16. Ibid., 38.

17. Ibid., 125.

18. Marty, *Pro and Con Book*, 43.

19. "Gladly," *US Catholic*, April 1978, 50–51.

20. Martin E. Marty, "The Electronic Church," *Missouri in Perspective*, March 27, 1978, 5.

21. Gallup and Poling, *Search for America's Faith*, 87.

22. Ibid., 86.

23. Ibid., 85.

24. Ibid.

25. Ibid., 18.

26. "Gladly," 70.

27. Gallup and Poling, *Search for America's Faith*, 16.

28. Ibid., 37.

29. Ibid., 15.

30. Ibid., 31.

31. Ibid., 19.

32. Ibid., 20.

33. Ibid.

34. Ibid., 32.

35. Ibid., 96.

DOCTRINE DIVIDES 10